W9-DIR-647

ᑭATE ᗷᑌᗴ

FIGHTING
BIOTERRORISM

Other books in the At Issue series:

FIGHTING BIOTERRORISM

Lisa Yount, *Book Editor*

Bonnie Szumski, *Publisher*
Scott Barbour, *Managing Editor*
Helen Cothran, *Senior Editor*

San Diego • Detroit • New York • San Francisco • Cleveland
New Haven, Conn. • Waterville, Maine • London • Munich

ST CHARLES COMMUNITY COLLEGE
LIBRARY
WITHDRAWN

© 2004 by Greenhaven Press. Greenhaven Press is an imprint of The Gale Group, Inc., a division of Thomson Learning, Inc.

Greenhaven® and Thomson Learning™ are trademarks used herein under license.

For more information, contact
Greenhaven Press
27500 Drake Rd.
Farmington Hills, MI 48331-3535
Or you can visit our Internet site at http://www.gale.com

ALL RIGHTS RESERVED.
No part of this work covered by the copyright hereon may be reproduced or used in any form or by any means—graphic, electronic, or mechanical, including photocopying, recording, taping, Web distribution or information storage retrieval systems—without the written permission of the publisher.

Every effort has been made to trace the owners of copyrighted material.

LIBRARY OF CONGRESS CATALOGING-IN-PUBLICATION DATA
Fighting bioterrorism / Lisa Yount, book editor.
p. cm. — (At issue)
Includes bibliographical references and index.
ISBN 0-7377-1611-8 (lib. bdg. : alk. paper) —
ISBN 0-7377-1612-6 (pbk. : alk. paper)
1. Bioterrorism—United States—Prevention. 2. Terrorism—Government policy—United States. I. Yount, Lisa. II. At issue (San Diego, Calif.)
HV6432.F54 2004
363.34'97—dc22   2003047236

Printed in the United States of America

Contents

Introduction

Most twentieth-century Americans found bioterrorism—the deliberate release of disease-causing microorganisms with the aim of causing devastating epidemics—unthinkable, perhaps even more so than nuclear war. Along with chemical warfare, biological warfare was forbidden by the 1925 Geneva Convention. More "civilized" nations regarded countries known to have tested biological weapons, such as Japan during World War II, with horror. To be sure, during the 1950s and 1960s, both the United States and the Soviet Union developed bioweapons programs—purely, they said, for defense in case the other side used such terrible weapons first. In 1969, however, President Richard Nixon formally ended the U.S. bioweapons program, and in 1972, the United Nations established the international Biological and Toxin Weapons Convention, in which all signatory nations pledged never to develop, produce, or stockpile such weapons. Both the United States and Russia signed it.

Confidence that no one would ever dare to use bioweapons began to be shaken during the late 1990s. After the collapse of the Soviet government in 1991, Ken Alibek (Kanatjan Alibekov), former deputy director of the Soviet bioweapons program, revealed that the program had continued long after 1972. Rumors circulated that some of the Soviet Union's bioweapons stock had fallen into the hands of smaller nations, such as Iraq and North Korea. The Clinton administration carried out simulation exercises for smallpox and plague attacks on civilian populations in 1999 and 2000, and Congress budgeted more than $1.5 billion specifically for bioterrorism preparedness in fiscal year 2000, more than double the amount allotted in the previous year.

The idea that disgruntled individuals or small groups as well as rogue governments might employ bioterror weapons also began to circulate around the start of the new century. Some writers called bioweapons "the poor man's atomic bomb" because they were easier and cheaper to produce than nuclear weapons. Experts pointed out that these smaller groups might not be deterred by factors that might limit the activities of national governments, such as fear of massive retaliation.

The most popular proposed bioterror microbe was the bacterium that causes anthrax, a disease usually confined to hoofed animals such as cattle and sheep but able to infect humans, often with fatal results. Anthrax bacteria were appealing because under harsh conditions they encase themselves in protective cocoons, forming spores that are almost impossible to destroy by methods that normally kill bacteria. Dried and ground into powder, such spores would be fairly easy for terrorists to distribute, and they would revert to their disease-causing form once they entered a human or animal body. In the late 1990s and early 2000s, letters or parcels supposedly containing anthrax spores appeared so often that an article in the July 1999 *Bulletin of the Atomic Scientists* called sending them a "hot new hobby." There were more than 150 anthrax incidents between March 1998 and July 1999 alone.

Every one of them, however, was a hoax. No one, it seemed, had actually been both willing and able to mail the deadly bacteria—and many experts doubted that anyone ever would. Some stressed that preparing and effectively distributing microorganisms as bioweapons required more technical skill and equipment than small groups were likely to possess. Others pointed out that there had been only one documented bioterror attack on American soil: In 1984, followers of cult guru Bhagwan Shree Rajneesh added salmonella bacteria to restaurant salad bars to sicken citizens in The Dalles, Oregon, so they would not vote in an election that the group wanted to influence. The attack made 751 people mildly ill but caused no deaths.

During the late 1990s and early 2000s, therefore, articles containing dire warnings about bioterrorism were matched by an almost equal number expressing powerful skepticism. For instance, W. Seth Carus, senior research professor and bioterrorism specialist at National Defense University, stated in a 1999 *New Republic* article that "the threat [of bioterrorism] is less compelling and not as imminent as often claimed." Similarly, Barbara Rosenberg, chair of the Federation of American Scientists Working Group on Biological Weapons, was quoted in June 2001 as claiming that "even those in high places in the military judge bioterror to be a low probability here in the U.S." Jonathan B. Tucker and Amy Sands, writing in the *Bulletin of the Atomic Scientists* in July 1999, attributed fear of bioterrorism to government exaggeration reinforced by "an obsessive fascination with catastrophic terrorism" in Hollywood films and popular novels.

Perhaps even more tellingly, most of the media, along with the bulk of the American public, ignored the bioterrorism issue entirely during this period. InfoTrac, a wide-reaching periodical database, cites only seventy articles on the subject between the database's earliest records in 1980 and the end of August 2001. John R. Hamre, head of the Center for Strategic and International Studies in Washington, D.C., himself was concerned about bioterrorism but admitted in April 2001 that it was "not something that average Americans worry much about."

Then came the terrorist airplane attacks on New York's World Trade Center on September 11, 2001—and three weeks later, Bob Stevens, photo editor for a supermarket tabloid in Boca Raton, Florida, entered JFK Medical Center in the nearby city of Atlantis suffering from chills and fever. Emergency room doctors thought he might have meningitis, a brain infection, but Larry Bush, the hospital's chief of staff and an experienced specialist in infectious diseases, looked at a sample of Stevens's spinal fluid under a microscope and made a far more startling diagnosis: anthrax. A Florida laboratory confirmed the diagnosis on October 4, and Stevens died a day later. Careful checks of his background and activities showed that there was no way he could have caught the disease naturally. Hours after Stevens's death, a man who had worked in the same building—the supervisor of the mail room—was admitted to a Miami hospital with what proved to be another case of anthrax. The unthinkable had become not only thinkable but real.

As the anthrax attacks continued and expanded over the next two months, bioterrorism became the year's third-hottest story, dwarfed only by the World Trade Center disaster and the war in Afghanistan. InfoTrac lists 545 articles about bioterrorism published during October and November alone. After the attacks had spread to major media offices in New York and closed down the office buildings of the U.S. Senate in Washington and had been shown to be spread by something that entered everyone's home—the mail—even respected NBC news anchorman Tom Brokaw signed off one night by saying, "In Cipro [the antibiotic being used to prevent and treat anthrax] we trust." Then and later, many opinions were expressed about what was being done or should be done to combat actual and potential bioterror attacks—but skepticism about the likelihood of such attacks was no longer among them.

The fall 2001 anthrax outbreak was a far cry from the apocalyptic scenarios envisioned in movies and government simulations. A mere twenty-one people caught the disease, and only five died. Nonetheless, this handful of individuals changed Americans' worldview forever because they were far from the only casualties of the still untraced attacks. Also severely stricken were an already-shaky economy, the U.S. postal system, and, perhaps most telling of all, the public's confidence that "it can't happen here." Ruth Levy Guyer and Jonathan D. Moreno wrote in *Social Education* in March 2002, "The anthrax events have done great physical damage to a small number of individuals. . . . The events have done great psychological damage to many more. Bioweapons were once the stuff of science fiction . . . today they are the realities of contemporary life."

1

The Bioterrorists:
An Overview

W. Seth Carus

W. Seth Carus is an expert on bioterrorism who has worked for the Center for Counterproliferative Research at National Defense University in Washington, D.C., as well as the Center for Naval Analyses. His writings include Bioterrorism and Biocrimes, *a history and analysis of bioterrorist attacks, from which this excerpt is taken.*

Analysis of past bioterrorist attacks can provide useful information about the types of groups and individuals who might carry out such attacks in the future. Most attacks so far have been the work of individuals or small groups and have occurred in the United States. Fewer than half have made use of known medical or scientific expertise. Bioterrorists are increasingly motivated by ethnic and religious aims as well as, or instead of, political aims, and have ideologies that justify causing mass casualties. Although they might be sponsored by hostile governments, they are often international groups with bases in many countries. They seldom advertise their intent in advance.

Editor's note: The following excerpt was taken from a study in which the author examined 269 alleged attacks involving biological agents that occurred in various parts of the world during the twentieth century. (The anthrax letter attacks of October 2001, thus, are not covered.) The cases Carus examined included criminal attacks committed for personal reasons as well as attacks with political motives. Of the 269 alleged cases, 191 were confirmed to have occurred. Eleven of these attacks allegedly involved governments. All the others were carried out by private individuals, small groups not affiliated with a government, or unknown parties.

In this [overview], characteristics of perpetrators who employed, acquired, or considered use of biological agents are examined. The perpetrators included in this study were both terrorists and criminals. Terrorists were groups who were motivated primarily by political objectives,

W. Seth Carus, *Bioterrorism and Biocrimes: The Illicit Use of Biological Agents Since 1900.* Washington, DC: Center for Counterproliferation Research, National Defense University, 2002. Copyright © 2002 by Fredonia Books. Reproduced by permission.

while criminals were driven by motives of financial gain, personal revenge, or some other non-political consideration.

Size of the perpetrating group

The size of the perpetrating groups was examined to gain some insight into the number of people required to exploit biological agents. Anyone participating in the acquisition or use of biological agents, whether in the planning, production, or distribution, was counted.

In three of the 180 confirmed non-state cases, the perpetrating group consisted of five or more people. All of these groups attempted use. There were 19 cases in which small groups of two to four people were involved. Generally, it appears that in small groups there was a single person with scientific or technical skills. Other members directed or supported the efforts of the sole expert.

A single individual was responsible for perpetuating plots in 43 cases. Significantly, the lone perpetrators successfully acquired biological agents in 19 of those cases, and used the agent in 12 of them. In 115 of 180 cases, there is not enough information available to estimate the number of people involved. In most such cases, the alleged perpetrators have never been identified.

Table 1: Size of perpetrating group

Type	Terrorist	Criminal	Other/ Uncertain	Total Cases
Lone	0	37	6	43
Small group (2–4)	5	12	2	19
Large group (5+)	3	0	0	3
Unknown	19	7	89	115
Totals	27	56	97	180

Geographical distribution

The perpetrators involved with biological agents have been located in countries around the globe. About 82 percent (147 of 180) of the cases took place in North America, all but one in the United States. Europe was the next most common location with 17 cases. Incidents occurred in Britain, France, Germany, Poland, and Russia.

Scientific and technical expertise

The range of perpetrator expertise varies considerably. Technical expertise could include background in medicine, microbiology, or pharmaceutics [drug manufacture].

The perpetrators had some scientific or medical training in 23 cases. In 16 of the cases, a physician or a Ph.D.-level microbiologist was involved. In several cases, individuals with medical training instigated use of bio-

Table 2: Geographic distribution				
Type	Terrorist	Criminal	Other/ Uncertain	Total Cases
North America	14	37	96	147
Europe	6	10	1	17
Asia	5	6	0	11
Africa	2	0	0	2
Australia/New Zealand	0	3	0	3
Totals	27	56	97	180

logical agents. A nurse, Ma Anand Puja, created the Rajneeshee biological warfare capability.[1] She relied on the expertise of a trained laboratory technician to culture the *Salmonella typhimurium* used to contaminate the salad bars. Dr. Suzuki, a Japanese physician and bacteriologist with considerable laboratory experience, infected at least 66 people with typhoid and dysentery before he was arrested in 1966.

In a few cases, the person who conceived the notion of using biological agents lacked the requisite skills, and so enlisted the services of unscrupulous physicians. Benoyendra Chandra Pandey drew on the medical skills of Dr. Taranath Bhatacharya, who was responsible for culturing the *Y. pestis* that was used in the 1933 murder of Pandey's brother. Similarly, in 1910 Patrick O' Brien de Lacy's brother-in-law was murdered by an injection of diphtheria toxin given by a physician, Dr. Pantchenko, who obtained the agent from a research laboratory in Russia.[2]

The available evidence suggests that in 36 cases the perpetrators had no scientific or medical expertise. Significantly, in only six cases is there any evidence that the perpetrators actually acquired biological agents. Equally significant, there is only a single case of use involving perpetrators with no known technical training, although this number might grow when more is known about some of the other perpetrators. In that case, Graham Farlow, a prison inmate, murdered a guard by injecting him with HIV-tainted blood. A perpetrator with no known professional training obtained a biological agent in only five cases. In three instances they extracted ricin toxin from castor beans, in one case used HIV-infected blood, and in the last case acquired the agent from a legitimate supplier. Eight of the 36 cases were extortion plots. Interestingly, only one extortion case involved a perpetrator who actually possessed a biological agent. The perpetrator in that case, Michael Just, had a Ph.D. in microbiology. He was convicted in 1996 for threatening to contaminate milk with *Yersinia enterocolitica*.

1. In 1984, followers of cult guru Bhagwan Shree Rajneesh added salmonella bacteria to restaurant salad bars to sicken citizens in The Dalles, Oregon, so they would not vote in an election that the group wanted to influence. The attack made 751 people mildly ill but caused no deaths.   2. The Pandey and O'Brien de Lacy cases were both murders carried out for private financial gain. Pandey took place in India in 1933 and involved injection of microorganisms that caused bubonic plague. O'Brien de Lacy took place in Russia in 1910 and involved injection of diphtheria toxin.

Table 3: Perpetrator expertise				
Type	Terrorist	Criminal	Other/ Uncertain	Total Cases
Medical or scientific expertise	4	17	2	23
No known expertise	6	24	6	36
Unknown	17	15	89	121
Totals	27	56	97	180

In 121 cases, the available evidence makes it impossible to assess the expertise of the perpetrators. Given that 91 of them were anthrax threats, all those cases probably involve people with no technical expertise.

Terrorist group characteristics

A number of studies have attempted to identify the characteristics of terrorist groups that could lead them to consider acquisition and use of biological agents. A study by Jeffrey Simon argues that a terrorist group inclined to use biological agents would demonstrate certain attributes:

- A general, undefined constituency whose possible reaction to a biological-weapons attack does not concern the terrorist group.
- A previous pattern of large-scale, high-casualty-inflicting incidents.
- Demonstration of a certain degree of sophistication in weaponry or tactics.
- A willingness to take risks.

These criteria are largely consistent with the characteristics of groups inclined to inflict mass casualties using biological agents. Simon's list may be less useful in identifying groups with alternative motives, such as harming agriculture, who may believe that they can deal with the risk of using biological agents that do not cause loss of life.

Another effort to consider the types of groups potentially attracted to the use of biological agents appears in a draft report on the threat of chemical and biological weapons prepared by the North Atlantic Assembly in 1996. That report gave the following list of terrorist groups likely to resort to biological weapons:

- Those whose goals include vague notions about world revolution, universalistic goals such as the Japanese Red Army and certain European radical left-wing groups.
- Those unconcerned with the effects of public opinion such as neo-Nazi groups in Europe and North America.
- Those with a history of high-casualty, indiscriminate attacks, such as Sikh extremists, pro-Iranian Shiite fundamentalist groups such as Hezbollah, and extremists within the Palestinian movement such as the Abu Nidal Organization.
- Those ideologically opposed to Western society in general.
- Those noted for their sophistication in weaponry or tactics, such as the Popular Front for the Liberation of Palestine-General Command.

• Those with state sponsors, especially where the sponsor is known to possess chemical or biological weapons.

This list is too inclusive to identify potential users of biological agents. It refers to groups that are not known to have considered use of biological agents, yet provides no basis for predicting under what circumstances a group might decide to adopt biological agents.

Later in 1996, Professor Walter Laqueur argued that terrorism is undergoing a profound change. In contrast to the politically motivated terrorists who predominated in the 1970s, many of today's terrorists define their objectives in ethnic or religious terms. Many of these groups are infected by millenarian ideas, believing that the world as we have known it is ending. Such groups may have few if any scruples about using weapons to cause mass casualties.

Other terrorism experts believe that the perpetrators most likely to employ biological agents are religiously motivated terrorists. Significantly, the two most significant bioterrorism incidents, involving the Rajneeshees and the Aum Shinrikyo, were undertaken by religious cults with political agendas. A former Chief of Counter-Terrorism at the FBI expressed a similar view of Middle East groups influenced by radical Islam.

> The danger originating from Middle East terrorist groups infused with the dogma of Radical Islamic Fundamentalism cannot be minimized. One of the principal concerns is the potential for their use of weapons of mass destruction. Given their demonstrated disregard for limiting casualties, indeed their apparent desire to inflict maximum damage, this scenario is one that has occupied much of the thinking of counter-terrorism planners at all levels of government. Biological and chemical weapons are certainly available to sophisticated terrorist organizations, especially those, like many of the Middle East groups, that operate with the support of governments. These weapons are both relatively easy to acquire and lethal in their application.

The essential consideration seems to be a combination of group's interest in causing mass casualty coupled with an ideology that would justify such operations. Such views are not necessarily unique to religiously motivated groups.

Domestic groups

There is considerable evidence to suggest that terrorist groups based in the United States have actively explored resort to biological agents. Experience suggests that interest in biological agents can come from a broad range of terrorist groups espousing radically different political philosophies. In the 1960s, the leader of the right-wing Minuteman group openly discussed the possibilities of biological agents, although there is no evidence that there was any substance behind the rhetoric. In the 1970s, several left wing groups considered bioterrorism. The quasi-Green R.I.S.E. was on the verge of disseminating several biological agents when the Chicago police arrested the ringleaders. The left-wing Weather Organization may have initiated a plot to acquire biological agents for use against municipal water systems. In the 1980s, a religious cult, the Rajneeshees, acquired and used biological agents. More recently, it appears that right wing groups, many affiliated with the militia movement, have expressed the most interest in biological terrorism. In some cases, the groups have acquired biological agents.

Fortunately, in the past there was more interest in bioterrorism than actual use. From this perspective, an important question becomes the extent to which domestic terrorists might decide to resort to biological agents. This involves two related considerations: to what extent could they acquire the capability to employ biological agents, and under what circumstances might they decide to use them?

About 82 percent of the cases took place in North America, all but one in the United States.

Although domestic groups could acquire some bioterrorism capability with little or no outside assistance, as demonstrated by the experience of the Rajneeshees, there is reason to doubt the ease with which such groups could cause mass casualties. Aerosol dissemination of biological agents may be beyond the capabilities of groups developing their own dissemination technology. Such groups would need to develop a considerable range of expertise, and it is likely that it would take some time before they could effectively undertake wide area dissemination of agent of highly lethal agents. Consequently, the initial uses of biological agents will probably involve small-scale actions with limited consequences. This suggests that effective public health surveillance of unusual disease outbreaks coupled with vigilant law enforcement activity could detect and respond to bioterrorism before the responsible groups develop a mass casualty capability.

The ability of terrorists to employ biological agents effectively would be greatly enhanced if such groups received external assistance from state-sponsored biological weapons programs. Such assistance could come directly from a state biological weapons program, or from individuals formerly associated with such a program.

State sponsorship

A number of countries with records of supporting terrorist organizations also are believed to have biological weapons programs. The Department of State names seven countries as state supporters of terrorism: Cuba, Iran, Iraq, Libya, North Korea, Sudan, and Syria. Published reports issued by the Department of Defense and the Arms Control and Disarmament Agency suggest that five of these countries, Iran, Iraq, Libya, North Korea, and Syria, possess biological warfare programs. Press reports have suggested that some Iraqi scientists associated with biological weapons research may be working in Sudan, and that the Sudanese have created a research institute for chemical and biological warfare funded by Osama bin Laden. Bin Laden is the former Saudi citizen who has become a major financial supporter for international terrorism. U.S. intelligence officials have reported that bin Laden has provided support for a Sudanese biological weapons program. This allegation was confirmed by the British Minister of State for Defence, George Robertson, in an on-the-record interview in 1998.

Since at least the late 1980s, press reports have claimed that Cuba has a biological weapons program. In early 1998, the Department of Defense expressed concern about Cuba's potential for creating biological weapons. Thus, almost all the countries associated with support for international terrorism also support efforts to develop biological weapons.

Relatively little publicly available information is available on the biological warfare programs of these countries, except for Iraq. What is known suggests that the sophistication of these programs varies considerably. Iraq certainly had a relatively sophisticated program, and until the war of 2003 probably retained a capability to develop biological weapons within a few weeks. Less is known about North Korea's activities, but it has been conducting research in the area of biological warfare for more than thirty years and probably has capabilities equal to or greater than Iraq's. Iran likely comes next in competence, followed by Syria and Libya. If it exists, Sudan's program is certainly the least developed.

Table 4: State supporters of terrorism and Bioweapons programs

State Supporters of Terrorism	BW Program
Cuba	Suspected
Iraq	Confirmed
Iran	Confirmed
Libya	Confirmed
North Korea	Confirmed
Sudan	Suspected
Syria	Confirmed

Sources: U.S. Department of State, *1996 Patterns of Global Terrorism Report: Arms Control and Disarmament Agency, Adherence To and Compliance With Arms Control Agreements, 1996*, as found at http://www.acda.gov, and Office of the Secretary of Defense, *Proliferation: Threat and Response*, November 1997.

Under what circumstances might a hostile state provide biological warfare expertise to a terrorist group? There is no evidence that such an exchange has ever taken place. In 1996, the Defense Intelligence Agency made the following points.

> Most of the state sponsors have chemical or biological or radioactive material in their stockpiles and therefore have the ability to provide such weapons to terrorists if they wish. However, we have no conclusive information that any sponsor has the intention to provide these weapons to terrorists.

Moreover, the Department of Defense asserted in 1997, "The likelihood of a state sponsor providing such weapons to a terrorist group is believed to be low."

In addition, it appears that terrorists in the 1990s relied less on state-sponsorship than was true in the 1980s. According to an unclassified CIA assessment, the primary threat increasingly comes from transient groups not necessarily dependent on any particular country for support:

> International terrorist groups have developed large trans-national infrastructures, which in some cases literally circle the globe. These networks may involve more than one like-minded group, with each group assisting the others. The terrorists use these infrastructures for a variety of purposes, including finance, recruitment, the shipment of arms and material, and the movement of operatives.

Potentially, the emergence of such transient groups has considerable significance. Such groups are less tied to the strategic interests of any particular country, and thus are less likely to act in a manner that reflects the guidance of specific countries. This makes them difficult to deter by exerting pressure on a state sponsor. While the groups may have substantial resources, they usually lack a permanent infrastructure, which may make it harder for them to generate an effective biological warfare capability. From this perspective, reports that bin Laden has financed a Sudanese biological warfare facility become a source of serious concern.

Political and moral constraints

Some analysts have argued that moral constraints are likely to inhibit use of biological weapons, either because the terrorists subscribe to moral tenets or because their supporters do. This is based on the argument, as articulated by terrorism expert Bryan Jenkins, that terrorists are usually not interested in mass murder.

> Simply killing a lot of people has seldom been a terrorist objective. Terrorists want a lot of people *watching*, not a lot of people *dead*. Most terrorists operate on the principle of minimum force necessary. Generally, they do not attempt to kill many, as long as killing a few suffices for their purposes.

Thus, Jenkins appears to argue that combinations of political and moral considerations have affected the willingness of terrorists to employ weapons that could cause massive harm. The implication is that they would be unwilling to employ biological weapons for the same reasons.

The Rajneeshees, for example, specifically rejected the use of a more dangerous pathogen, *S. typhi*, which causes typhoid fever. However, in this case, the primary factor that militated against use of the agent was not moral qualms, but rather concern that an outbreak of typhoid fever would attract too much attention. The group believed that it could accomplish its intended objective, incapacitation, using a generally non-lethal agent, *S. typhimurium*, which causes a common form of food poisoning.

In fact, in the late 1990s and beyond there has been growing evidence that terrorist groups are interested in causing mass casualties. This is reflected in the publicly expressed views of the CIA.

> The emphasis on high casualty operations and the frequency

of attacks on nonofficial targets have been significant trends in international terrorism in recent years. These trends are reflected in the statistics on international terrorism, which show that the number of terrorist incidents has declined during the 1990s but casualties from terrorist attacks lately have been on the increase.

We expect these trends to continue. The newer breed of international terrorist, who seeks revenge more than carefully defined political objectives, is interested in inflicting mass casualties.

Thus, there are growing concerns of erosion in the political and moral constraints that in the past kept most terrorist groups from resorting to weapons of mass murder.

In general, however, the most serious constraint on the use of biological agents has probably been operational rather than moral. For many purposes, biological agents are more difficult to use and less effective than other weapons. Guns and bombs are probably more than sufficient if the objective is to murder one or even several hundred people. The fact that so many individuals and groups have considered using biological agents is an indication of the fragility of the moral barriers.

Operational considerations

The research highlights certain operational aspects in the use of biological agents. While these observations should be considered tentative, because they are based on a small sample, they are derived from real world experience.

Terrorists or criminals who possess or use biological agents almost never advertise their intent. In only one case is it clear that perpetrators known to have possessed biological agents sent commmuniqués or otherwise made known the fact of possession. In contrast, those who claimed to possess biological agents almost never did. This tends to suggest that individuals or groups who do not claim credit will undertake most cases involving actual use of biological agents.

A number of countries with records of supporting terrorist organizations also are believed to have biological weapons programs.

This experience adds weight to the views of some experts that terrorists are increasingly unlikely to claim credit for their actions. According to Bruce Hoffman, "Terrorists now deliberately seek to conceal their responsibilities for attacks in hopes of avoiding identification and subsequent arrest." In Hoffman's view, terrorists can obtain the publicity that they seek even without claiming credit for specific acts of terror. Significantly, he argues that this anonymity may make them more likely to commit increasingly lethal acts.

Hiding biological weapons programs is easy. The efforts of the Rajneeshees to develop biological agents were detected only when the cult fell apart and law enforcement agencies developed informers among former members of the group. An intensive public health investigation of the outbreak failed to determine the cause of the outbreak. In fact, an Oregon State official issued a report claiming that unsanitary practices by restaurant workers caused the outbreak and dismissed allegations that intentional contamination was a factor. It was only a year after the outbreak that law enforcement officials developed credible evidence that intentional contamination was responsible.

There are growing concerns of erosion in the political and moral constraints that in the past kept most terrorist groups from resorting to weapons of mass murder.

The available evidence suggests that intelligence and law enforcement agencies are unlikely to learn that a particular terrorist group is interested in acquiring and using biological agents. This is a concern of the intelligence community, as reflected in the publicly stated views of the State Department's Bureau of Intelligence and Research.

> The involvement of terrorist groups in WMD [weapons of mass destruction] would be difficult to detect. This is particularly true with regard to chemical and biological materials since the agents can be obtained fairly easily and the production can be hidden.

There is no evidence that Japanese authorities were aware of Aum Shinrikyo's interest in biological agents.[3] Only after the subway attack did Japanese law enforcement officials learn of the biological warfare program and hear the allegations that Aum actually attempted to use biological agents. Moreover, the Aum was virulently anti-American, and repeatedly accused the United States of waging chemical and biological warfare on the cult. Yet, the U.S. intelligence community was completely unaware of its activities. Neither the Central Intelligence Agency (CIA) nor the Federal Bureau of Investigation (FBI) appears to have believed at the time that they had any responsibility for tracking such activities on the part of groups like the Aum.

---

3. Aum Shinrikyo was a Japanese religious cult. On March 20, 1995, they released a nerve gas called sarin into the Tokyo subway system, killing twelve people and sending a total of about five thousand to hospitals. They also attempted several attacks using biological weapons between 1990 and 1995, but all of these attacks failed.

2

The United States Is Not Prepared for a Bioterror Attack

Scott Gottlieb

Physician Scott Gottlieb is a resident fellow at the American Enterprise Institute and a staff writer for the British Medical Journal.

The slowness with which the Centers for Disease Control and Prevention identified the West Nile virus, a virus newly transmitted to the United States by natural means, suggests that the agency will also have trouble identifying the cause of a bioterror attack in time to prevent disaster. Such an attack is likely to feature viruses, which are easy to engineer, produce, and spread. Lack of a comprehensive system for early detection of outbreaks of infectious disease could make bioterror attacks hard to spot. One possible mode of detection is to note increases in appearance of people with certain symptoms in emergency rooms, but some experts feel this method is not very reliable. A better method might be virus testing of blood samples gathered in the normal course of medical diagnosis, but public health officials are unlikely to accept this technique.

In August 1999, four New York City residents showed up at hospital emergency rooms complaining of headaches and dizziness. A few became paralyzed. Doctors were stumped. Botulism? A rare nerve inflammation? Scans eventually revealed that the patients all had encephalitis—an inflammation of the brain.

Eight cases and another two weeks later, the Centers for Disease Control (CDC) came up with a diagnosis: St. Louis Encephalitis, a viral disease transmitted by mosquitoes. Publicly, the CDC and local health agencies stuck with their diagnosis. Privately, scientists were skeptical: They tested mostly for standard diseases, not rare ones.

CDC scientists continued their research. Doctors didn't crack the case until birds started to die at the Bronx Zoo. An astute veterinarian sent a few bird brains to a friend at the Department of Agriculture. The samples

Scott Gottlieb, "Wake Up and Smell the Bio Threat," *American Enterprise*, vol. 14, January/February 2003, pp. 26–27. Copyright © 2003 by American Enterprise Institute for Public Policy Research. Reproduced by permission of The American Enterprise, a magazine of Politics, Business, and Culture. On the web at www.TAEmag.com.

ended up at CDC headquarters in Atlanta, where scientists used genetic fingerprinting to discover that it was West Nile Virus—never before detected in North America—that was making people sick. By autumn, a total of 62 people had been diagnosed with the virus, and six had died.

But less than one of every 100 people infected with West Nile actually becomes seriously ill. Only mosquitoes can spread it. America's next viral outbreak, whether natural or an act of bio-terrorism, may not be so easy on us. The official response to West Nile instills little confidence that disaster could be avoided in the case of a bio-terror attack. In early 2003, everything America has that was designed specifically to counter bioterrorism is old, expensive, and slow.

Surveillance: Too little, too late

The greatest threat probably comes from viruses: They are relatively easy to engineer into designer bio-weapons. Technicians can produce viruses from a rather small collection of DNA. (In July 2002, scientists reported they had created the polio virus from recipes available on the Internet.) Many viruses can also survive for long periods of time outside living cells, especially in a dry state, where they can easily become airborne. There are no antiviral drugs that have the same striking effectiveness and broad attack range that antibiotics do.

Indeed, we might not even know that an attack had occurred for some time. Most bio-terror experts worry about the silent release of an infectious agent of which we have no hint until the incubation period has passed and the terrorists have fled. Then people would come to emergency rooms with non-specific symptoms that may not immediately trigger the right medical diagnoses. So what's required is a good early warning system. Right now, disease surveillance comes in two principal forms. Passive surveillance usually calls on doctors to take the initiative to report suspicious medical cases to state health authorities. Active surveillance asks public health officials to contact doctors directly to gather the data. Both methods share one inherent handicap: By the time people go to the hospital, an epidemic could have already broken out.

Everything America has that was designed specifically to counter bio-terrorism is old, expensive, and slow.

Except for food- and water-borne diseases, the U.S. has no comprehensive system for detecting outbreaks of infectious diseases before people start to get ill. Each state decides which diseases to report to the state health department and which information to pass on to the CDC. Often, chaos results. "There's so much noise, we can hardly pick up the signal," says Frederick Burkle of the Defense Threat Reduction Agency at Johns Hopkins University. Even worse, we don't even have the needed technology: About half of state labs can't do the type of genetic testing that ultimately unearthed West Nile.

A bit of progress has been made: The CDC is encouraging local public health leaders to develop systems for surveying the public for worrisome signs such as unusual diagnoses or spikes in doctor visits—a practice public health officials call syndromic surveillance. New York City has such a system in place: Emergency rooms feed data into a central computer system; software alerts public health officials when it finds clusters of symptoms in one geographic area, unusual combinations of symptoms, or inordinately high numbers of symptoms reported by a particular hospital. Health officials hope to couple these systems with databases that track over-the-counter drug sales (patients often purchase medicine before they decide to go to the emergency room).

Syndromic surveillance is swiftly becoming a mainstay of bio-terror preparedness nationwide. It has also prompted a rash of false alarms, as doctors, trained to spot these syndromes, leap to conclusions they would never have considered before 9/11 [the terrorist attacks on the World Trade Center and the Pentagon on September 11, 2001]. On August 4, 2002, an emergency room doctor at Beth Israel Hospital in Brooklyn decided that a patient with fever and a skin rash fit the description for smallpox. He activated New York's emergency response system over what turned out to be a mild case of contact dermatitis [an allergic reaction affecting the skin].

Health officials could detect infections before people develop symptoms.

And there is much skepticism about the approach. "Syndromic diagnosis—that's nothing but a big charade," says Dr. C.J. Peters, former head of the CDC's top security lab. "By the time you start getting blips in emergency rooms, it's too late."

President [George W.] Bush has pledged $11 billion for 2003 and 2004 to reconfigure the infrastructure of the national health system. The federal government has already spent more than $3 billion to upgrade disease surveillance, expand laboratories, and improve communications abilities. But all of these measures won't much strengthen our ability to detect unusual microbes.

Testing blood for viruses

Health officials still focus on tracking downstream markers of disease, the things that happen after people get sick—medicine purchases, strange clinical syndromes, doctor visits. Instead, surveillance systems need to be geared to spotting the microbes themselves, before people have incubated and spread these germs. Some scientists want to develop means for routinely screening blood for the myriad viruses ranging from influenza to designer bugs terrorists might develop. If this kind of surveillance existed, it could provide a national trip-wire for new viral pathogens.

How would it work? Health officials would collect samples of serum from all the blood that ordinary diagnostic labs dispose of daily. A national lab would screen the samples for viruses. That way, health officials could detect infections before people develop symptoms, allowing for quarantines and early medical interventions to control impending epidemics.

This idea is the brainchild of Norman Anderson, a celebrated researcher in vaccine purification and clinical testing who heads the Viral Defense Foundation, and his son Leigh Anderson, the former chief scientific officer at the biotech firm Large Scale Biology. The technology already exists to sequence viruses' DNA—a technique called shotgun sequencing. It was pioneered by Craig Venter, the former chief executive of Celera Genomics, which mapped the human genome in record time, and has become the mainstay of genomic research. The Andersons' proposal would involve checking each blood sample for viruses and then comparing them to a computer database of known viruses around the world. (It's a similar technique that ultimately led scientists to discover that West Nile Virus was behind the deaths in New York.) Computers could keep count of what has been found in a particular blood sample, and assemble a human virus index to monitor the ebb and flow of different diseases in the population. Any DNA sequences that the computer didn't recognize could be flagged for bio-terrorism monitors. If this technology sounds futuristic, it's not. In 2003, oceanic researchers already employ similar procedures to separate viruses from ocean water.

To get a representative sample, researchers would probably need to take blood only from a select group of labs, not all of them. Right now, CDC researchers call up a pre-selected group of doctors scattered across the country to check for any unusual medical cases. This system relies on doctors to spot the early signs and symptoms of something more sinister than ordinary influenza. West Nile proved this kind of surveillance slow, and too unreliable to thwart outbreaks. By going straight to blood, the CDC can have early and incontrovertible data.

Alas, public health officials by their very training are averse to such technological solutions, placing their faith in statistics and epidemiology. But these techniques suffer from poor sensitivity, lack of timeliness, and minimal coverage. America's public health establishment must realize that biological weapons exist. As biology moves from a laboratory to a digital science, even unsophisticated hacks can develop dangerous weapons. As terrorists bring increasing sophistication to their craft there's a growing disproportion between our defensive technologies—developed to thwart ordinary illnesses—and the bio-weapons.

The threat of smallpox looms large in 2003, and policymakers are debating how many vaccine doses to make available. Iraq and North Korea, among others, probably have smallpox samples that could be turned into weapons. If smallpox were released into our cities, officials might have only a few hours to react. By the time the virus is first detected, it could have already spread to hundreds or thousands of close contacts. Sick people will have boarded planes to distant locations, coughed their way through closed buildings, or ridden on subways. That's how pandemics start.

3

The United States Is Committed to Fighting Bioterrorism

George W. Bush

George W. Bush was elected the forty-third president of the United States in November 2000. Prior to that, he was governor of Texas. He gave the following speech in Pittsburgh on February 5, 2002.

The government is proposing to provide $1.6 billion in funds for state and local governments to help hospitals and others improve their ability to respond to bioterrorist attacks. It also plans to develop new tests and treatments for potential bioterror weapons such as anthrax and smallpox. The proposed budget will contribute a total of almost $6 billion to defense against bioterrorism, an increase of more than 300 percent. This expenditure will benefit the health system as a whole as well as strengthening defense against bioterrorism.

Homeland defense takes many forms. One, of course, is to secure our borders, to make sure we understand who's coming in and out of our country. Part of making sure America's safe is to have as good information as possible about what takes place in our ports of entry. That's why I spent a little time in Maine the other day, talking about how we're going to boost the presence of the Coast Guard, for example, to make sure our border and our homeland is as secure as possible.

Part of having a secure homeland is to have a good airport system that's safe for people to travel; an airport system that is inspecting bags by inspectors who are qualified to inspect bags. Part of a homeland defense is to have good intelligence sharing between the federal, the state and the local level. Part of a homeland security is to have a first responders mechanism that's modern and current. And part of homeland security is to be prepared to fight any kind of war against bio-terror.

And that's what I want to spend some time talking about today. Some of us remember that back in the '50s we had what was called the DEW

George W. Bush, speech given at the University of Pittsburgh's Masonic Temple, February 5, 2002.

[Distant Early Warning] line on the Arctic Circle, to warn us if enemy bombers were coming over the North Pole to attack America. Well, here in Pittsburgh, I had the honor of seeing a demonstration of the modern DEW line, a Real-time Outbreak and Disease Surveillance system, developed right here, which is one of the country's leading centers on monitoring biological threats.

What we saw was how to take real data on a real-time basis to determine if there was an outbreak of any kind, including a terrorist attack. The best way to protect the homeland is to understand what's taking place on the homeland so we can respond. And so the modern-day DEW line to me was fascinating. And I appreciate those who have worked so hard to come up with an incredibly useful tool for America, a useful tool to protect ourselves.

It's an investment that will pay off not only for better security, but for better health.

I also appreciate the fact that the University of Pittsburgh and Carnegie Mellon Institute launched what's called a biomedical security institute to help protect the nation in all ways from the insidious biological attack.

You know, I've come to realize—having spent some time in Pittsburgh and particularly hearing the briefings today, that while Pittsburgh used to be called "Steel Town," you need to call it "Knowledge Town." There's a lot of smart people in this town. And I'm proud to report to my fellow citizens, they're working in a way to make America safe. A lot of money, obviously, comes from the state government for that. We are grateful. But the federal government has a role to play, as well.

I'm proud to say the Department of Defense, the Centers for Disease Control and Prevention, the Department of Health and Human Services all provide financial support to the Biomedical Security Institute. But, as you can tell from reading the papers and tell from my . . . State of the Union address, I have made the homeland security a top budget priority, and I asked Congress to respond in a positive way to this request.

For example, we're asking for $1.6 billion. This is additional money for state and local governments to help hospitals and others improve their ability to cope with any bio-terror attack. One, it's important to be able to recognize what's happening; and, secondly, we've got to respond, respond in a modern way, a way that will help the American people survive any attack if it were to come.

I want to make sure that each region around the country has the proper equipment and the right amount of medicine for the victims of any attack, should it occur. We've got to upgrade our communications, not only between the federal government and the state government, but between state governments and local communities, and between counties and local jurisdictions. We've got to be able to talk to each other better, so that there's real-time communications, so that we can share information in a crisis. Information-sharing will help save lives. And so part of the money is to bring our systems up to speed, to make them more modern and more responsive.

New tests and treatments

The budget also adds $2.4 billion to develop new test protocols and new treatments for bio-terror weapons. We were able to save lives during the anthrax outbreak of 2001 but some infections were identified too late, and some people were too badly infected to save. We must do everything in our power, everything to protect our fellow Americans. We need better testing, better vaccines, and better drugs if America is going to be as safe as it can possibly be.

And there's some hopeful news. Scientists tell us that research we do to fight bio-terrorism is likely to deliver great new advances in the treatment of many other diseases, such as tuberculosis, pneumonia, malaria and HIV/AIDS. The monies we spend to protect America today are likely to yield long-term benefits, are likely to provide some incredible cures to diseases that many years ago never thought would be cured. It's an investment that will pay off not only for better security, but for better health. And I ask Congress to support me on spending this money.

We're also going to expand our nation's stockpile of antibiotics and vaccines. We're going to have more of these important antibiotics and vaccines readily available. By the end of the fiscal year, we'll have enough antibiotics on hand to treat up to 20 million people for anthrax, plague and other bio-terrorist diseases. We're preparing for the worst. We'll provide funds to states to make sure they can distribute medicines swiftly. And we're also going to expand our bio-terror intelligence service. During the Korean War, we created what was called an Epidemic Intelligence Service (EIS) to help defend America if any of our Cold War enemies tried to use bio-weapons against us. Now we need to adapt the EIS to a new era and to a new mission. We'll make the commitment to expand and modernize the service, and to work with scientists in this country and friendly nations around the world.

All in all, my budget will commit almost $6 billion to defend ourselves against bio-terrorism—an increase of over 300 percent. It's money that we've got to spend. It's money that will have good impact on the country. It's money that will enable me to say that we're doing everything we can to protect America at home.

4

U.S. Agriculture Is Vulnerable to Bioterror Attacks

Mark Wheelis, Rocco Casagrande, Laurence V. Madden

Mark Wheelis is a microbiologist at the University of California, Davis, with an interest in the history of biological warfare and scientific aspects of chemical and biological arms control. Rocco Casagrande works for Surface Logix, Inc., and is interested in the development and testing of devices to detect and analyze biological weapons. Laurence V. Madden is a plant pathologist at Ohio State University, Wooster, who specializes in the epidemiology of plant diseases.

A bioterrorist attack on agriculture—deliberate introduction of animal or plant diseases—does not have the headline-grabbing power of other types of attack, such as an induced smallpox epidemic, but it could produce immense economic damage, especially through effects on exports. Attempts at containment would create further losses. Agroterror attacks are easier to carry out than attacks on humans and require relatively little technology and expertise. Outbreaks could be induced in many places at once. In addition to the usual religious and political motives for terrorist attacks, agricultural terrorists might be driven by motives such as moral objections to genetically modified foods or mistreatment of animals on intensive farms. U.S. programs to detect and control agricultural disease outbreaks need to be aggressively strengthened.

Most of the concern in the 1990s about U.S. vulnerability to bioterrorism has focused on terrorist use of pathogens to attack the civilian population. This concern increased in the wake of the September 11, 2001, terrorist attacks on the World Trade Towers and the Pentagon and the anthrax letter attacks on U.S. Senate offices and the media. However, a number of analysts have pointed out that terrorist attacks on livestock or crops, although unlikely to cause terror, are also a concern because they could be executed much more easily and could have serious economic consequences. It is worth considering the consequences for the U.S. economy had there been a widespread and sudden outbreak of foot-and-mouth disease (FMD) shortly after September 11. The stock market

Mark Wheelis, Rocco Casagrande, and Laurence V. Madden, "Biological Attack on Agriculture: Low-Tech, High Impact Bioterrorism," *Bioscience*, vol. 52, July 2002, pp. 569–77. Copyright © 2002 by American Institute of Biological Sciences. Reproduced by permission of the Copyright Clearance Center, Inc.

probably would have plunged even further, and its recovery could have been significantly delayed. More substantial consequences are easy to imagine. This article will give an overview of U.S. vulnerability to agricultural bioterrorism and biocrimes. . . .

Economic effects

The burden on agriculture of endemic and naturally imported epidemic disease is high, confirming the capacity of animal and plant diseases to cause economic harm. The United States is free of many globally significant livestock diseases because of effective surveillance of herds and imports and aggressive eradication campaigns. Even so, approximately $17.5 billion are lost each year because of diseased livestock and poultry. In general, losses from animal disease account for 17% of the production costs of animal products in the developed world and nearly twice that amount in the developing world.

The total cost of crop diseases to the U.S. economy has been estimated to be in excess of $30 billion per year. The costs include reduction in the quantity (e.g., reduced bushels per acre) and quality (e.g., blemished fruit, toxins in grain) of yield; short-term costs of control (e.g., cost of purchasing and applying pesticides) and long-term costs (e.g., development of resistant varieties of crops through breeding and development of new pesticides); extra costs of harvesting and grading diseased agricultural products (e.g., separating diseased from disease-free fruit); costs of replanting blighted fields; costs of growing less desirable crops that are not susceptible to the dominant plant pathogens in an area; higher food prices; unavailable foods; trade disruptions; and public and animal health costs caused by the production of toxins by some plant pathogens.

In contrast to the sweeping campaigns undertaken to eliminate the most virulent diseases of livestock, efforts generally have not been made to eradicate diseases of crops. One goal of plant disease control has been to maintain most indigenous diseases at a low or very low incidence level through a range of management techniques. The exception is when a disease has a very narrow geographic distribution (as would a newly introduced exotic disease), spores are not dispersed great distances, and disease incidence is low. In such a situation, eradication may be feasible.

A successful [agroterror] attack could have severe economic consequences.

Despite the high toll endemic disease and periodic incursions of epidemic disease exact on agriculture, many pathogens have not appeared in the United States at all, while others have made only very rare appearances, and still others were eradicated decades ago (especially with animals); many of these are considered to be serious threats to agriculture. Thus, the exotic, highly contagious pathogens causing these diseases could be chosen as bioweapons for the large economic consequences that could result from their introduction. Pathogens that cause diseases such as FMD, rinderpest, African swine fever (ASF), soybean rust, Philippine downy mildew of maize, potato wart, and citrus greening could, if introduced into the continental United States, have serious consequences for the U.S. economy.

Even a massive outbreak of plant or animal disease in the United States would not cause famine; the agricultural sector is too diverse, too productive, and too closely regulated for that to be a realistic possibility. However, a successful attack could have severe economic consequences. The most substantial impact would be the loss of international markets for animal or plant materials. Member nations of the World Trade Organization are entitled to ban imports of plant or animal materials that may introduce exotic diseases into their territories. Thus, importing countries that are themselves free of a particular highly contagious animal or plant disease will routinely impose sanitary or phytosanitary [plant quarantine] restrictions on trade with countries in which that disease breaks out. This can result in billions of dollars of lost trade.

Under some circumstances, a pathogen could be effectively introduced without the perpetrators entering the country.

For instance, as soon as the first case of FMD was reported in the United Kingdom in 2001, the European Union (and other countries) immediately blocked imports of British beef, sheep, and swine and products derived from them. The total sum of lost revenues from contracted international markets has not yet been determined in July 2002, but it will certainly be billions of dollars. For the United States, with $41 billion of beef, $19 billion of dairy, and $14 billion in pork sales annually, the trade consequences of an outbreak of FMD could be much larger. A 1999 study of the impact that an outbreak of FMD would have on California agriculture concluded that losses, using conservative estimates, would be $6 billion to $13 billion even if the outbreak were contained within California and eradicated within 5 to 12 weeks.

Karnal bunt of wheat, caused by the fungus *Tilletia indica*, provides another example of severe economic consequences caused by agricultural disease. About 80 countries ban wheat imports from regions with karnal bunt infections, even though the disease does not have a large direct effect on crop yield. When the disease was discovered in Arizona and surrounding areas in 1996 (probably from an accidental introduction from Mexico), there was an immediate threat to the overall $6 billion per year U.S. wheat crop, since about 50% of produced wheat is exported. Because of this threat, the Animal and Plant Health Inspection Service (APHIS) of the U.S. Department of Agriculture (USDA) immediately mobilized efforts to contain the outbreak within the original small area and to eradicate the disease. From 1996 to 1998, APHIS spent over $60 million on the effort, and growers in this small affected area lost well over $100 million from lost sales and increases in production costs. In this case, the localized nature of the outbreak allowed the United States to convince its trading partners that none of the contaminated wheat was entering the market, and wheat exports continued from the rest of the country.

Unfortunately, karnal bunt was discovered again in 2001, this time in Texas, and a new round of containment and eradication efforts has been initiated.

In addition to the political and religious ideological motivations for terrorism, agriculture provides some new ones.

In some cases, domestic demand can also be significantly affected. Even minor outbreaks of disease that can potentially infect people can have severe economic consequences. Since September 11, 2001, a mere three cases of mad cow disease have been found in Japan; yet as a consequence, Japanese beef sales dropped approximately 50% during this period.

In addition to the costs that result from reduced international and domestic demand, the costs of containment can be quite substantial, as the examples discussed above make clear. Thus, even for commodities that are not exported in large amounts, an outbreak of disease that provokes vigorous eradication efforts may have a substantial economic effect. Taiwan, for instance, spent about $4 billion in an unsuccessful effort to eradicate FMD after it was introduced to the country in 1997.

Containment, eradication, or control?

As demonstrated in the examples above, introductions of exotic pathogens that cause highly contagious animal or plant diseases may elicit rapid and aggressive attempts to contain and eradicate them and these measures commonly cause more economic damage in the short term than the disease itself. Despite the costs, such intervention is often justified, since if exotic highly infectious diseases become endemic, the long-term costs would be much greater than the costs of containment.

Containment and eradication of exotic animal diseases is commonly done by culling all potentially exposed animals to break the chain of transmission. Thus, small numbers of infected animals can lead to the slaughter of large numbers of healthy ones. Many of the animal diseases that are potential bioterrorist threats are caused by viruses, for which there is no practical therapy once the animal is infected. Therefore, transmission cannot be interrupted by treatment, but only by culling diseased and exposed animals or by vaccination (when that is an option—see below). In contrast, about 75% of plant diseases are caused by fungi, and these can be controlled, with varying degrees of effectiveness, by the application of fungicides. For many high-value-per-acre crops (e.g., fruit and vegetables, ornamentals), fungicides are used in routine control of endemic diseases. Some fungicides actually move systemically within plants and can arrest the infection process during the early phases of infection. More commonly, however, fungicides are applied to the surface of plants and are used prophylactically to provide short-term protection from fungal infection. When an introduced disease is discovered, infected and possibly exposed plants are culled ("rogued"), and fungicides can be used to treat plants in surrounding areas (even for low-value-per-acre plants) to prevent infection. This method is expensive, it fails to prevent all infections, and it can have negative environmental consequences.

Transmission of bacterial and viral crop diseases is difficult to control with chemical pesticides, unless such diseases are transmitted by insect vectors, in which case insecticides may be useful. Because of these difficulties, containment and eradication of bacterial pathogens depend heavily on quarantining infected areas and removing all infected and exposed plants.

The only chance of successfully containing and eradicating a crop pathogen is to start the process relatively soon after introduction, when the focus of infection is small, there are few infected individuals, and the dispersal distance of spores is short. For some diseases, such as rust of several crops (e.g., stem rust of wheat, caused by *Puccinia graminis f. sp. tritici*), spores can be dispersed very long distances (thousands of kilometers), so the spread of disease can be substantial before the pathogen is discovered. For these reasons, eradication is generally not attempted.

Ease of agroterror attacks

One of the reasons that a bioterrorist attack on human populations is difficult is that the development of an effective bioweapon is a technically daunting task. Many of the antipersonnel agents that have been used as weapons ("weaponized") are poorly transmitted among humans (e.g., anthrax), so a large amount has to be disseminated at once to cause large numbers of casualties. The only effective way to infect large numbers of people simultaneously is to generate a respirable [breathable] aerosol. However, aerosol preparation to a particle size that is effective in causing inhalational disease is quite difficult, and once so prepared, it is highly hazardous to the perpetrators themselves (unless they are vaccinated and taking prophylactic antibiotics).

Other anti-human agents are contagious (e.g., *Yersinia pestis*, the causative agent of plague), but they too have to be disseminated in large quantities for widespread infections, because agent transmission can be interrupted by antibiotic treatment. Since organisms as *Y. pestis* do not form the highly resistant spore form that *Bacillus* [*anthracis*, the bacterium that causes anthrax] does, it is technically quite challenging (and dangerous) to prepare a large stockpile of the agent. Still other agents are viral rather than bacterial, and their preparation and weaponization is even more challenging because of the more demanding technologies needed for laboratory culture.

In some special situations, highly contagious viruses could be effectively introduced by voluntarily infected terrorists who would travel to the target area during the incubation period of the disease. This reportedly was done a number of times in the 1950s and 1960s in an effort to infect Native Americans in the Matto Grosso of Brazil, by land speculators who would be able to purchase tribal lands once the natives no longer inhabited them. However, in the developed world, for any disease other than smallpox, it is unlikely that such a low-tech method would be effective. Thus, the technical expertise required to mount a mass-casualty biological attack on the human population is formidable and probably beyond the capabilities of most terrorist groups (and indeed of many nations). However, the anthrax infections in late 2001 have clearly shown that only a few cases are sufficient to produce a large psychological impact on the population.

Unfortunately, the same difficulties do not exist for many of the diseases that would make effective agricultural bioterrorist weapons. These diseases of animals and crops are highly contagious and spread effectively from a point source, as the 2001 FMD outbreak in the United Kingdom dramatically confirms. Moreover, humans can safely handle the causative organisms, with no risk of becoming infected. None of the plant pathogens of concern, nor most of the animal pathogens, cause disease in humans. Thus, there is no need for vaccination, prophylactic antibiotic use, or special precautions to prevent infection of the perpetrators.

Although a small outbreak may not produce a large psychological impact (relative to a single person dying of anthrax or smallpox), several of these pathogens owe much of their economic impact to trade sanctions that are imposed in response to a few cases; thus, even small outbreaks can have very large economic effects. A few cases of FMD scattered around the country could interrupt much of U.S. animal product exports for several months, even if the outbreaks were promptly contained (importing countries would want to wait several weeks or months to verify that the outbreak was truly contained before resuming imports). Obviously it is technically easier to cause a few scattered cases of disease than to prepare a kilogram-sized stockpile of weaponized agent for aerosol distribution.

> *Since agricultural bioterrorist attacks cannot be prevented altogether, an effective response plan to minimize the effects is essential.*

Material to initiate an outbreak of plant or animal disease therefore does not have to be prepared in large quantity—a few milligrams could be sufficient to initiate multiple outbreaks in widely separated locations—if the goal is to disrupt international trade, or if the terrorists are sufficiently patient to allow a crop disease to develop over several months by transmission from individual to individual. And the agent does not necessarily have to be grown in the laboratory or otherwise manipulated—a small amount of natural material taken from a diseased animal or plant can serve without any additional manipulation. For instance, a few hundred microliters of scrapings from the blistered mucosa of an FMD-infected animal, or blood from an animal hemorrhaging from ASF, or a handful of wheat tillers heavily infected by the stem rust pathogen can provide more than enough agent to initiate an epidemic. Such materials are readily available in many places in the world where the diseases of concern are endemic, and they can be obtained and transported without any particular expertise other than what is necessary to recognize the disease symptoms with confidence. Since only small amounts are needed, they can be easily smuggled into the country with essentially no chance of detection.

Dissemination of many introduced pathogens likewise requires relatively little expertise. Animal virus preparations could be diluted and disseminated with a simple atomizer in close proximity to target animals, or the preparation smeared directly on the nostrils or mouths of a small number of animals. This could be done from rural roads with essentially no chance of detection. Dissemination of animal diseases could also be done surreptitiously at an animal auction or near barns where animals are densely penned (as in chicken houses or piggeries). For plant diseases, simply exposing a mass of sporulating fungi [fungi giving off spores] to the air immediately upwind of a target field could be effective, if environmental conditions were favorable for infection. The biggest challenge of introducing a plant pathogen is probably timing the release with the appropriate weather conditions. If pathogens are released immediately before the start of a dry period, few, if any, infections are likely to result. However, if released at the start of a rainy period, these pathogens could cause a major epidemic.

Rapid and accurate diagnosis is the cornerstone of effective control, but comprehensive planning for response is also required.

The technical ease of introducing many agricultural pathogens makes it more likely that terrorists or criminals would release pathogens in several locations in an attempt to initiate multiple, simultaneous outbreaks. This would ensure that trade sanctions would be imposed, because it would undermine any argument that the outbreaks are localized and do not jeopardize importing countries. It would also be more likely to overwhelm the response capacity and lead to the uncontrollable spread of disease. This is the principal way in which a bioterrorist attack would differ from a natural disease introduction, and it raises the question whether a system designed to respond to natural introductions can deal effectively with sudden, multifocal outbreaks.

Under some circumstances, a pathogen could be effectively introduced without the perpetrators entering the country. This is, of course, true of crops planted on both sides of an international border, such as sorghum along the Mexican border or wheat and barley along the Canadian and Mexican borders. These crops have experienced disease outbreaks that spread from acreage outside the United States—sorghum ergot, karnal bunt of wheat, and barley stripe rust, for example. Thus, such pathogens could be deliberately introduced in an adjacent country, a potential advantage to a terrorist if disease surveillance and control programs were less effective there. Multiplication of the pathogen in the foreign acreage could lead to large numbers of spores blowing across the border and initiating an outbreak that could very quickly become very large. International movements of animals also provide opportunities for the introduction of an animal pathogen without the perpetrator having to enter the country. For instance, the very serious 1997–1998 outbreak of classical swine fever in the Netherlands was due to inadequate disinfection of a swine shipment from Germany. However, this is an unlikely route for bioterrorist attack, because its effectiveness requires a failure of quarantine or disinfection procedures.

International trade in nonliving agricultural materials can also introduce disease. An example is the 2000 outbreak of FMD in Japan, which occurred simultaneously in two widely separated locations. Investigation suggested that at least one of these locations was infected by straw imported from China (where the FMD virus is endemic) and used as bedding for cattle. Although this particular event appears to have been natural, it shows that deliberate contamination of materials such as bedding or fodder could initiate simultaneous outbreaks at widely scattered locations, making containment extremely difficult. The invasive Asian long-horned beetle, a pest of trees, probably arrived in the United States from China via a similar route, from eggs laid in wooden packing material. If this pest becomes established in the United States, the damage to fruit, lumber, and tourism industries is expected to exceed $40 billion. For crops, seeds present similar vulnerability. Many plant pathogens either infect or reside on seeds, and a considerable (and increasing) amount of seed for U.S. crops is produced outside the United States.

Finally, there is a substantial moral difference between killing people and killing plants and animals, and a corresponding difference in the intensity of expected law enforcement response and legal consequence. Thus moral norms and legal consequences can be expected to constitute less of a disincentive to the agricultural bioterrorist than to the bioterrorist who targets people.

Motives for terror

We normally think of a terrorist attack as being ideologically motivated, and this is certainly one motive for attacking the agricultural sector. The immense potential for economic damage could make this kind of attack attractive to enemies of the United States, particularly because it is relatively easy and safe for the perpetrators. Given the escalating scale of terrorist attacks on the United States, this is cause for serious concern.

In addition to the political and religious ideological motivations for terrorism, agriculture provides some new ones. There is considerable opposition to the increasing use of genetically modified (GM) crop plants and domestic animals, which have been largely developed in the United States and are most widely used here. For instance, GM soybeans accounted for 63% of the crop grown in the United States in 2001. Worldwide, over 130 million acres are planted with GM crops, because they possess increased resistance to herbicides or insects. The United States alone cultivates almost 70% of the total acreage of GM crops. Opposition to the use of GM crops and animals has sometimes taken the form of vandalism and destruction, and it is quite possible that some activists will at some point turn to diseases as weapons to attack GM organisms. Radical animal rights groups may wish to attack animal agriculture to prevent corporations from profiting from animal suffering. Ingrid Newkirk, president of People for the Ethical Treatment of Animals, stated recently that she openly hoped "that it [FMD] comes here [the United States]. It will bring economic harm only for those who profit from giving people heart attacks and giving animals a concentration camp–like existence. It would be good for animals, good for human health, and good for the environment."

Attacks on the agricultural sector could also be motivated by greed, properly termed "biocriminality" rather than bioterrorism. The major shifts in agricultural markets and commodity prices that could result from a successful attack could provide such economic motivation. Profit could be made by the manipulation of futures markets, selling short the stock of major agrochemical companies, or intentionally sabotaging overseas competitors to capture lost import markets. For instance, outbreaks of FMD have changed global dominance in the export of pork. In the 1980s, Denmark supplied most of the pork imported by Japan. After a 1982 FMD outbreak halted pork exports from Denmark, Taiwan filled Japan's need for pork and continued to be its primary supplier even after Denmark was declared free of FMD. After the 1997 FMD outbreak in Taiwan, the United States captured the Japanese pork market and continues to supply Japan with most of its imported pork. Corporations, individuals, organized crime groups, and even national governments might be attracted to the very large financial gain that is at least theoretically achievable from the judicious use of plant or animal diseases to manipulate markets or commodity prices.

Another possible motive is revenge. The United States and the United Nations Drug Control Program have supported research and development of the use of plant pathogens for killing or reducing yields of opium poppy, coca, and cannabis. The programs involved selection of virulent strains of fungi, consideration of large-scale production of fungal spores, and testing of the most efficient ways of delivering the spores. The work is exactly analogous to the anticrop biological weapons programs of the former Soviet Union and the United States during the cold war. Because of various political and social pressures, these programs are on hold or moving very slowly. However, if the deliberate release of plant pathogens to destroy drug crops did ever go ahead, there could be a powerful incentive for those in the illicit drug business to retaliate by releasing plant pathogens into U.S. crops.

Preparing for attacks

In response to a 1998 Presidential Decision Directive, and especially to the attacks on September 11 and the subsequent anthrax infections, considerable effort is now being expended to reduce the vulnerability of the United States to bioterrorist attack. A small part of this effort is aimed at protecting crops and livestock. Among other things, a National Research Council committee is evaluating the vulnerability of U.S. agriculture to biological attack and determining strategies for dealing with that vulnerability. USDA and other federal departments and agencies are in the process of making many changes, and it is premature to comment on their effectiveness. However, it is worth making a few general points and sketching the scientific agenda as we see it.

Aggressive counterterrorism measures and greater international intelligence sharing can be expected to reduce the likelihood of a bioterrorist attack on agriculture. Severe criminal penalties may also act as a deterrent. The 1989 Biological Weapons Antiterrorism Act prohibits the development, production, and stockpiling of biological agents for use as a weapon, and it explicitly applies to anti-plant and anti-animal agents. Violation incurs penalties up to life imprisonment. Nevertheless, no measures, singly or in combination, can eliminate the threat. And a bioterrorist attack on the agricultural sector, because of its relative ease, safety, and minimal technical requirements, is probably less likely to be deterred than an attack on human targets. Since agricultural bioterrorist attacks cannot be prevented altogether, an effective response plan to minimize the effects is essential. Knowledge that the United States can respond quickly and effectively to terrorist attacks, and can minimize their impact, would itself serve as an additional deterrent.

An effective response to an agricultural bioterrorist attack is in principle no different from effective response to a natural introduction of exotic diseases. The differences are largely quantitative: A bioterrorist attack is more likely to be multifocal, and it is more likely to begin explosively (because larger numbers of pathogens could be initially involved). These considerations suggest that at a minimum, existing response strategies should be evaluated and improved to deal with the more demanding outbreak situations that would most likely result from a bioterrorist attack.

However, there is good reason to question whether our existing response capabilities are adequate even to deal effectively with fully natural disease introductions. The experience of the United Kingdom in 2000 and Taiwan in 1997 with FMD, or the Netherlands with classical swine fever in 1997–1998, shows that even developed countries with advanced agricultural health services can be overwhelmed by some outbreaks. This suggests that more radical changes in the way we approach outbreak control may be necessary.

Identifying disease

Effective preparation for a bioterrorist attack has several components. Probably most important is early detection. However, U.S. farmers, veterinarians, plant pathologists, and agricultural extension agents are generally not well prepared to rapidly identify exotic animal and plant diseases. Thus a significant educational task confronts us. It is hard to overestimate the importance of that task; even a couple of days' delay in identifying an exotic animal disease can mean the difference between an easily controllable outbreak and one that escalates out of control because of rapid transmission. The UK FMD outbreak is thought to have been as serious as it was largely because of the failure to identify infected sheep for more than a week, during which time the sheep were transported and the disease spread throughout the country.

For crop diseases, there is an additional problem: Crops are grown over millions of acres, and there is no way of carefully observing a very large proportion of individual plants. The first plants with symptoms typically are observed only after substantial spread has already occurred; 0.1% or more of the plants in an area may need to be infected before symptoms are first noticed. This may be too late for successful eradication, especially for highly contagious diseases such as rusts, which have spores that travel long distances. Long-term efforts are needed to develop strategies and technologies to reduce the time to discovery.

Confirmation of a diagnosis of most of the diseases of concern is done with accurate, sensitive molecular techniques, but samples may have to be shipped across the country, consequently delaying confirmation of a diagnosis for days. Expanded local capacity, at least at the state or regional level, to diagnose relevant exotic diseases is therefore important. Complicating the problem, diagnostic laboratories for plant pests (diseases and insects) are typically run by land grant universities and state departments of agriculture. These are often underfunded and understaffed, and they may not have the facilities or supplies to run molecular or biochemical assays or to provide rapid turnaround times. These labs need to be better supported to deal quickly with exotic pathogens.

A single serious outbreak prevented or quickly controlled could pay for the program several times over.

Beyond the need to expand local capacity is the necessity that diagnostic technology be able to detect diseased animals or plants before they are symptomatic or contagious. This will be especially important after a disease outbreak is established and intensive containment and eradication efforts are being pursued. This would allow earlier culling of infected herds or fields, thereby greatly limiting pathogen transmission. It would also allow the culling of exposed herds or fields to be delayed until there was evidence of infection, since there would then still be time for culling before further disease transmission occurred. These measures could dramatically reduce unnecessary culling and thus reduce containment costs. Such technology has been developed for FMD, for example, but it is not yet widely available.

Diagnosis of presymptomatic plants is practical only for systemic diseases, those in which the pathogen is transported throughout the plant by the vascular tissue. Many threatening plant pathogens, however, are not systemic, and infection is localized; in these cases, tests on samples of plant material will not reliably detect infection. This limitation to presymptomatic diagnostic testing has hindered eradication efforts for citrus canker, a bacterial disease discovered in Florida in 1995 that has global quarantine significance.

Controlling outbreaks

Rapid and accurate diagnosis is the cornerstone of effective control, but comprehensive planning for response is also required. Many of the decisions about control strategies can be (and should be) made in advance, so that action can be taken immediately upon notification of an outbreak. Response plans obviously will be specific for each disease of concern. For animals, these will be almost exclusively diseases on List A of the Office International des Epizooties. However, for crops, there is no worldwide consensus on the most threatening pathogens that could be used as biological weapons. Developing a consensus for a list of the major bioterrorist threats is thus the first priority in protecting crops. Such a list is necessary to guide the development of surveillance plans, diagnostic tests, and response plans for best containing and eradicating an introduced pathogen.

Probably the most important technical development for animal disease control would be to develop effective vaccines for all diseases of concern. FMD vaccines, for instance, are each protective against only one of the various strains of FMD virus, and they give only limited protection, requiring revaccination every six months or so. A polyvalent [affecting several strains of disease-causing microorganisms], long-lasting vaccine could provide valuable control options. Vaccines also need to be designed such that a vaccinated animal can be reliably distinguished from a previously infected animal, because seriological [blood test] evidence is used to document disease-free status for the purpose of international trade. These vaccines could be donated to international efforts for disease control, thereby keeping stockpiles renewed, production capacity busy, and the risk of importation of disease low.

Control strategies for crop diseases depend on the epidemiology of the particular disease and on the cropping system. For field crops such as wheat, for example, breeding for resistance is a fundamental approach for control of many diseases. However, breeding is done only for endemic diseases, because it is too expensive to develop resistant varieties for pathogens that are not present. Clearly, efforts must be made to at least identify sources of resistance for threatening pathogens so that the time it takes to develop new varieties is reduced. Genomics should speed this process considerably through the eventual development of plant cultivars that have general resistance to multiple plant pathogens.

Genomic technologies should also facilitate the development of a new generation of pesticides that combine high specificity, high effectiveness, and low environmental and health risks. Because plant disease control will very likely continue to rely heavily on pesticide use, substantial research and development efforts are warranted, including genome sequencing of important current and potential pests and their hosts.

The United States currently responds to large outbreaks of agricultural disease by deploying teams of specialists to assist in the diagnosis, containment, and eradication of the disease. There are too few of these teams in the United States to effectively control a large or multifocal outbreak of highly contagious disease (as would probably be the case with an intentional disease introduction). Having more of these teams would increase our capability to respond quickly and effectively to large disease outbreaks, whether the outbreak is intentionally or unintentionally caused.

Because the United States normally has few outbreaks of disease that require such a response, these teams could be deployed internationally to combat disease outbreaks. This international deployment would have several benefits. The members of these teams would gain valuable experience in the diagnosis and containment of diseases that do not often occur in the United States, experience that they could not otherwise acquire. These internationally deployed professional teams could limit the extent of serious animal diseases in other countries, thereby diminishing the chances of an accidental introduction of that disease into the United States and minimizing the opportunities for a terrorist to obtain the pathogen from the environment. Plant diseases, for reasons discussed above, are less likely to be eradicated or contained globally, and thus the benefits of international deployment of specialists may be less obvious for them. Even so, the experience the teams gain would be valuable in itself, and the humanitarian benefit to developing countries would bring valuable goodwill.

A justified expense

Despite our best efforts, this country will continue to be vulnerable to deliberate introductions of exotic plant and animal diseases by terrorist groups with an ideological agenda or by governments, corporations, or individuals with a profit motive. The vulnerability to agricultural bioterrorist attack is a consequence of the intrinsically low security of agricultural targets, the technical ease of introducing consequential diseases, and the large economic repercussions of even small outbreaks. It is exacerbated by structural features of U.S. agriculture that are unlikely to change without forceful government intervention: low genetic diversity of plants and animals, extensive monoculture, and highly concentrated animal husbandry.

While the vulnerability cannot be eliminated, effective response can minimize the damage from both intentionally and naturally introduced disease. We have suggested an aggressive scientific agenda: continuing education programs for farmers, veterinarians, and extension specialists; development of new diagnostics, vaccines, and pesticides; development of new sensing technologies for early identification of plant disease outbreaks; development of plant varieties resistant to diseases not yet endemic; and an increase in the number of outbreak control specialists assigned to international disease control efforts. This is an expensive agenda, but cost-effective in context—a single serious outbreak prevented or quickly controlled could pay for the program several times over. Given the ever-increasing international traffic in agricultural commodities combined with decreasing transit times, we can expect continued natural introductions of exotic plant and animal diseases. These will easily justify the cost of the programs that we recommend. Clearly, aggressive action is warranted to address the deficiencies of our current response system, for both naturally and deliberately introduced plant and animal diseases, given the billions of dollars at stake.

5

Protection of U.S. Agriculture Against Bioterror Attacks Has Been Strengthened

Michael A. Gips

Michael A. Gips is a senior editor of Security Management, *a magazine published by the American Society for Industrial Security.*

Deliberately induced outbreaks of animal disease, like natural ones, can cause economic devastation, and bioterrorist attacks on livestock would be relatively easy to carry out. However, the U.S. Department of Agriculture and other groups are taking steps to reduce U.S. agriculture's vulnerability. Border inspection for diseases and other problems is being increased. Farmers are being taught how to report animal disease and reduce the physical vulnerability of their farms. Veterinary and other programs aimed at early detection of outbreaks are being launched or strengthened. New communication networks are being created. Difficulties in containing outbreaks revealed by simulations are being addressed. Security is being increased at laboratories working with microorganisms that cause animal diseases.

B usiness was moving briskly at one of the sale barns in rural Kansas where farmers market their cattle. Then the on-site veterinarian noticed some cattle with lesions on their tongues—a symptom of foot-and-mouth disease. Although the vet didn't suspect foot and mouth, he followed protocol and notified state and federal authorities. Lesion samples were quickly flown to the Foreign Animal Disease Diagnostic Laboratory in Plum Island, New York. Within 48 hours, the diagnosis was back: negative.

Though the cattle ended up posing no risk (it turned out that they had merely eaten hay containing thorns), observers watching as the vets performed their ministrations took their concerns about a potential out-

Michael A. Gips, "The First Link in the Food Chain," *Security Management*, vol. 47, February 2003, pp. 40–47. Copyright © 2003 by ASIS International, 1625 Prince Street, Alexandria, VA 22314. Reproduced by permission.

break to the media. When accounts of these suspicions were broadcast, panic ensued and the cattle futures market plummeted. Eventually the truth came out, but not until the cattle industry took an estimated $50 million hit.

As this 2001 incident shows, even the suspicion of animal disease can rock the U.S. economy, which is why the hundreds of such investigations conducted annually by federal authorities are not usually publicized. An actual outbreak of disease would cause an exponentially more severe disruption as England learned when bovine spongiform encephalopathy—mad cow disease—was found in its cattle stock in the late 1980s. Panic spread across the world in 1996 when the British government suggested that the disease could be transmitted to humans. Five years later, the British livestock industry was devastated once again, this time by foot-and-mouth disease. It is this potential for causing severe economic disruption that could make agrobusiness in the United States an attractive target for al Qaeda or other terrorist groups.

With awareness of terrorism at unprecedented levels and Britain's mad-cow and foot-and-mouth crises fresh in the public's memory, government agencies in the United States, along with farm interest groups, academics, and farm industry personnel in 2003 are collectively attempting to beef up U.S. livestock and poultry security. While protecting the food chain is important from pasture to package, perhaps nowhere is security more crucial than well prior to processing, including at the borders, on the farm, at auctions, and in government laboratories. Major efforts involve border security, farmer education, disease diagnosis and surveillance, rapid reporting, disease containment, and lab security.

The risks

Experts agree that an attack on livestock wouldn't be the most efficient or lurid way to cause human casualties. "Terrorists gravitate toward visually glaring and strong pictures," points out Peter Chalk, Ph.D., a policy analyst for RAND. "Killing cows probably doesn't fulfill that kind of mindset." In addition, many animal diseases have no real effect on humans.

But infecting cattle, pigs, sheep, or other animals with diseases such as foot and mouth or mad cow is likely to erode public confidence in food safety and devastate the U.S. agricultural industry, which relies heavily on exports. The U.S. livestock industry alone is worth an estimated $100 billion, and economic disruption—affecting markets in corn, soybeans, leather, shipping, pharmaceuticals, and so on—could be worth far more.

Other experts note that an attack against livestock would be relatively easy to pull off. According to Jeff Bender, assistant professor in veterinary public health in the College of Veterinary Medicine at the University of Minnesota, so-called Category A agents—several of which can be transmitted to humans, such as plague and Ebola—are easily disseminated, though difficult to acquire.

Routine vaccinations do not address at least 22 diseases; they include bluetongue (a virus affecting sheep and cattle), rinderpest (another virus affecting sheep and cattle), and avian [bird] influenza. Such harmful biological agents abound around the world; according to the World Directory of Collections of Cultures and Microorganisms, harmful agents are retained in 450 repositories located in 67 countries, including Iran and China. These bacterial, viral, and toxic agents can be transmitted by air, water, and food.

Moreover, farm animals' living conditions are conducive to the rapid spread of disease. Feedlots can hold up to 100,000 head of cattle, and poultry production units can house ten times that amount of birds. Dairies keep thousands of milking cows in close proximity. Steroids and stress have lowered these animals' resistance to viral and bacterial infections, according to officials at the U.S. Department of Agriculture (USDA).

Jan Sargeant, an associate professor of epidemiology at Kansas State University (KSU), says that the U.S. agricultural industry could be a victim of its own efficiency. She notes that trade in animals at auctions and livestock markets has the potential for spreading disease from one farm to many others. County fairs and horse shows also contribute to the problem, says James Roth, professor of veterinary microbiology and preventive medicine at Iowa State University.

Even the suspicion of animal disease can rock the U.S. economy.

In October 2001, the Research Division of the National Association of State Departments of Agriculture (NASDA) issued a critique on the USDA's agrosecurity efforts. The report pointed out that, while the department's Animal and Plant Health Inspection Service-Veterinary Services (APHIS-VS) "has so far been successful in carrying out its mission," APHIS-VS suffers from inadequate facilities, understaffing, lack of training, outdated surveillance techniques, poor communication, and insufficient employment of new technologies. The report then issued 152 discrete recommendations. For example, it called for the creation of a national surveillance director leadership position to oversee a national surveillance system and the extension of USDA authority to inspect private boats and aircraft arriving from foreign countries.

The National Academies' National Research Council also weighed in on U.S. defenses against agroterrorism. In its report, issued in September 2002, the council warned that the United States is vulnerable to bioterrorism, largely because it can't detect and identify many pathogens and cannot quickly respond to a large-scale attack. The council issued many of its own recommendations, such as the development of a list of biological elements that could potentially be used.

With additional government funding, APHIS-VS has begun to assess and address the NASDA recommendations and others, according to Valerie Ragan, assistant deputy administrator for APHIS-VS. "We've been working pretty aggressively on it," she says. Specifically, the 152 recommendations were divided into seven categories and assigned to discrete working groups: national surveillance system, laboratory systems, exclusion activities, coordinated response, organizational dynamics/communication, information technology, and veterinary accreditation. APHIS-VS is working with many other state and federal agencies. "Partnership building is a key theme of getting this all accomplished," she says.

Other measures have been taken to strengthen the system as well, says Floyd Horn, an administrator at the USDA's Agricultural Research Service. He points out, for example, that in the late 1990s the U.S. government banned the feeding of nerve tissue to cattle, while British officials decided not to. Consumption of such nerve tissue has been linked to mad-cow disease which, of course, ravaged the United Kingdom but did not enter the United States. APHIS-VS and the beef industry deserve major credit for that, Horn says.

Border security

APHIS-VS has long paid close attention to foreign animal disease outbreaks and their potential to enter the United States. But the country's extensive borders have made flagging disease a difficult task. In fact, the National Research Council's September report notes that neither foreign imports nor foreign visitors are screened for biological threats at the borders of the United States.

But several policy makers and academics say that much more work needs to be done. Jerry Gillespie, director of the Western Institute for Food Safety and Security, University of California-Davis, doubts that the border screening effort for agricultural diseases is effective. California, with a big, sophisticated agriculture industry and vast borders accessible by land, sea, and air, is particularly vulnerable, he says.

After 9-11 [the terrorist attacks on September 11, 2001], and with the creation of the U.S. Department of Homeland Security (DHS), more resources are being devoted to this issue. Specifically, APHIS has significantly expanded the number of inspectors posted at borders. Moreover, many—perhaps all—of these officers will now report to the DHS. In addition, APHIS has been working on monitoring wildlife disease on the Mexican border, and it is considering possible collaboration with the Mexican government.

"We have a lot of opportunity to improve the way we monitor the borders," he says. One such opportunity is the school's efforts to work with APHIS and the Food and Drug Administration to come up with more "imaginative" ways to detect problems at the border.

An attack against livestock would be relatively easy to pull off.

Some experts have suggested starting the screening process overseas, as has been proposed for cargo inspections. But not everyone agrees with the emphasis on inspections, regardless of where the process is conducted. For example, Rocco Casagrande, an agroterrorism expert who works for a company that develops new drugs, has suggested that funding should instead go to U.S. veterinarians to receive overseas training to hunt down and study exotic diseases. Not only would this help U.S. officials recognize these diseases, Casagrande contends, but it would also limit the disease duration and thus reduce the chances of these diseases getting a foothold in the United States. A possible collateral benefit might be that such a humanitarian program could reduce the possibility that an aggrieved person would attack the United States in the first place, he adds.

Education

Besides the proverbial fox in the henhouse, farmers traditionally haven't had to worry much about security, and they have, therefore, never been educated about threats and countermeasures. With the rising threat to U.S. agriculture, industry groups have been rushing to bring farmers up to speed, but progress has been slow.

A survey of farmers by the Extension Disaster Education Network (EDEN), a group of educators across the United States who share disaster management experiences and strategies, indicates that only 14 percent of 312 respondents believed they were prepared for agroterrorism. Almost two-thirds of the respondents said that they either lacked access to educational information on agroterrorism or were unaware whether they had access. Three-quarters of respondents said that they had not "made considerable investments" to make their farms more "biosecure." (These numbers reflect survey responses as of early January 2003.)

What should farmers be aware of? They need some knowledge of reporting issues, financial aid, and physical security vulnerabilities, say experts.

Reporting. First, farmers must learn the importance of rapid disease detection and response, says Steve Cain, director of agriculture communications at Purdue University, West Lafayette, Indiana. Purdue is trying to help disseminate this type of information through EDEN.

Financial aid. Farmers also need to know the extent to which they will be financially compensated for quarantine expenses, lost sales, and other costs, says Purdue's Cain. In early 2003, regulations for indemnity reimbursement by the federal government already cover certain animal diseases, but more may be covered soon. Cain says that farmer buy-in will hinge on their understanding and acceptance of a compensation scheme.

Gary Weber, executive director for regulatory affairs of the National Cattlemen's Beef Association, says that APHIS-VS has been making significant advances with regard to farmer compensation. He says that his organization has been working with APHIS to make sure that the government's indemnity program is fair and that farmers get paid quickly. Specifically, APHIS proposes a system that will make it clearer to farmers how the value of livestock is assessed. Also, Weber says, APHIS is moving towards paying 100 percent of the value of each animal that has to be destroyed; in early 2003, he says, the federal government pays half, with state governments and industry expected to cover the balance. Farmers often appeal the award amounts, which has slowed the depopulation process, he says. Full federal compensation should eliminate that problem.

Physical vulnerabilities. Physical vulnerability detection (followed, of course, by appropriate countermeasures) is a major goal of farmer awareness efforts as well. Joe Miller, a regulatory specialist for livestock for the American Farm Bureau Federation (AFBF), says that the AFBF has been advising farmers to keep track of who is on their property. The AFBF has also been encouraging farmers to create ties with local law enforcement and prosecutors to speed their response to a potential problem on the farm. The goal is for the farmer to tell officials how the farm works and to develop a mutual trust so that if the farmer calls for help, law enforcement will know that it is a serious concern, says Miller.

Mike Doyle, director of the University of Georgia's Center for Food Safety, has also been championing awareness efforts. For example, Doyle has been working with the dairy industry to alert farmers about the vulnerability of bulk tanks that hold milk. Since these tanks combine the milk of many cows, a single infected cow could taint a whole tankful of product. Doyle is also working on methods of killing such bacteria; heating is the typical method, but that might not be enough with an "unusual" agent, he says.

In addition, farmers need to be educated about the appropriate physical security measures they should take. Physical security goals to protect farm animals predominantly involve keeping trespassers—who could taint water, feed, or the livestock itself—off the property and to secure these food and water sources. Industry groups and government offices, including the Minnesota Department of Agriculture and the American Feed Industry Association (AFIA), have issued guidelines for protecting feed, agricultural chemicals, dairy foods, and other items.

Early detection

If prevention fails, the next important step would be early detection. David Bossman, president of the AFIA, notes that contaminating a load of feed "wouldn't have a particularly broad effect" if it was detected soon enough. Once identified, infected animals could simply be slaughtered. "But if it gets into the meat supply and it gets to the press, that's the horror story," he says.

Educating veterinarians and public health officials is a major component in ensuring timely detection of animal illnesses and preventing their spread. Before ill animals can be diagnosed, private-sector and government veterinarians alike must understand what they are seeing. But according to RAND's Chalk, veterinary schools have often failed to teach students how to spot early signs of foreign animal diseases.

That's changing. Iowa State's Roth notes that, with a grant from the USDA, the school has established a Web-based course in exotic animal diseases for veterinary students. He says that the program will be made available to all U.S. veterinary schools in 2003. Soon, he says, the course will also be available to practicing veterinarians.

Dr. Corrie Brown, a veterinary pathologist with the University of Georgia College of Veterinary Medicine and an advisory member of the U.S. Secretary of Agriculture's Committee on Foreign Animal and Poultry Diseases, is also focused on raising veterinarians' awareness. She says that her school is helping the U.S. Animal Health Association put the latter's authoritative work on foreign animal diseases on the Internet and on CD-ROM. CDs will be sent free of charge to every veterinary school in the country, she says, as well as to any practitioner who requests one.

Brown also notes her school's efforts at boosting accreditation requirements for veterinary schools. She and her colleagues prodded the American Veterinary Medical Association's council on education to change its accreditation guidelines so that each college must prove that it is teaching foreign animal diseases. "That is a huge step forward," she says.

In summer 2002, the University of Minnesota launched a three-week class on biosecurity and biosafety for executive-level professionals pursuing a master's of public health administration, says the school's Bender. As part of the course, veterinarians, state agricultural officials, pharmaceutical company representatives, and others visited farms, focusing on threats to the swine and dairy industries. "We showed them critical control points for those industries," Bender says.

In addition, APHIS-VS has been training staff veterinarians and other key outside veterinarians in foreign animal disease recognition at its Plum Island facility.

Communication

Even if diseases are recognized, the danger must be quickly communicated. "The number one issue is to have rapid diagnostic systems available that are connected nationally," says Norman Cheville, dean of the College of Veterinary Medicine at Iowa State University.

Cheville's school is one of 15 facilities that have received federal support to create a rapid automated diagnostic network. Dubbed the National Animal Health Laboratory Network, the chosen facilities are basically pilots to see how quickly they can communicate with one another, says APHIS's Ragan. (Such a network was called for in the NASDA report. The National Research Council's report also called for a lab network to rapidly identify and detect agents posing a high threat.) The system is expected to be rolled out later in 2003. It will require users to enter and upload information about local outbreaks; the data will be automatically analyzed for any trends.

Harley W. Moon, a veterinary professor at Iowa State and the chairman of the council that drafted the NRC report, was heartened by the Department of Agriculture's creation of a diagnostic network but questioned whether it will be carried through. "The question now is whether it will be sustained," says Moon. "If it only lasts a year, it won't be worth it." APHIS's Ragan points out that "funding is being developed as we're moving along. There's no magic pot of money out there now."

Farmers . . . have . . . never been educated about threats and countermeasures.

Other federal efforts are going into ensuring coordinated communication of surveillance and diagnosis efforts. For example, APHIS-VS recently appointed Ragan national surveillance coordinator to pull together different programs and to oversee the programs of the 50 states. These actions also reflect recommendations made by NASDA in its October 2001 report.

Another significant federal development has been the deployment of disease-identification technologies in state and federal labs, according to the USDA's Horn. One system, by Idaho Technologies, is called the Ruggedized Advanced Pathogen Identification Device (RAPID). This portable unit identifies agents within minutes and can transfer this information securely online to a central database. Cepheid [a company in Sunnyvale, California, that makes biological detection systems] makes a related technology also being tested in government laboratories. (Both of these products use reagents—substances used to help to identify other agents—developed in significant part by USDA's Agricultural Research Service and Tetracore, Inc., says Horn.) Because the United States is a signatory to an international agreement governing animal health issues, these two technologies must pass the scrutiny of the Paris-based World Organisation for Animal Health, known by its French initials OIE, before they can be used, says USDA's Horn.

At the state level, with the support of APHIS-VS, KSU's Sargeant is helping to roll out a program that will keep Kansas veterinarians keyed in on real-time information about animal diseases. Kansas State is setting up a central database and outfitting about 15 veterinarians in the state with a personal digital assistant, with cell phone and digital imaging capacity, equipped with special software that was originally used at Sandia National Laboratories to detect disease outbreaks in humans.

The vets will use the devices to send reports of cattle symptoms they witness to the database. After this test run to fine-tune the system, plans are to equip every vet in Kansas with such a device and move beyond cattle to other animals. "Veterinarians can get real-time feedback," Sargeant says. "That should encourage them to enter data." The program, funded by the Kansas Department of Animal Health, may also be tried in Nebraska, and other states may follow suit.

If diseases are recognized, the danger must be quickly communicated.

Other logistical changes can help speed early detection. For example, Cheville notes that testing for animal diseases has been moving from federal to state labs. For example, UC Davis's Gillespie says that California has started relying more heavily on its sophisticated state labs, even though it still meets a federal obligation to ship specimens to a designated lab on Plum Island. Use of local labs is important because it saves precious shipping time, he says. He adds that other states are also realizing the time savings of instate examinations: "States are asserting themselves; they're saying to federal authorities, we can't wait around for you,'" Gillespie says.

In Minnesota, meanwhile, the Center for Animal Health and Food Safety at the University of Minnesota has been coming to the aid of an overburdened state system. In response to a recent West Nile outbreak that outstripped that state's ability to respond, the school provided veterinary students to collect and report dead birds as well as to remove their brains for state lab analysis, according to Bender. Students and staff also contributed to epidemiology efforts, especially with horses and birds. Physically, state agencies could not handle that surge, especially over a summer period," Bender says.

Other innovations are being studied. For example, Casagrande mentions the possible use of air sensors in cattle feed lots or other areas where farm animals are housed together. Since viruses spread via exhalations,

Casagrande says, these sensors will immediately be able to identify any airborne viruses. Such an approach has been tested in Britain, he says, with the sensors detecting foot-and-mouth disease two days before it otherwise would have been discovered.

Containment

Once a disease is identified and communicated, it must be contained and isolated. Recent simulations have shown the difficulty in doing that.

For example, Cain said that Purdue underwent an exercise with state police, public health officials, state veterinarians, environmental groups, and others in which a fictitious disease similar to foot and mouth forced the quarantine of a hog farm. Indiana state police had to enforce the quarantine, a massive task that outstripped the department's ability to respond.

"The size of the farm isn't as much of an issue as is movement of animals to other farms," observes Cain. "Some farms birth and wean hogs and ship them to other farms," he says, from which they are often sold to still other farms.

Cain says that the exercise showed that the economic impact of an epidemic striking farm animals would be massive, including $7 million to contain the disease, $700 million in animals that would have to be euthanized, and a potential $7 billion hit to the U.S. economy. This last figure, though speculative, reflects potential export sanctions as well as the loss that would be incurred if crops were not sold to farms as animal feed (an estimated two-thirds of U.S. corn production feeds farm animals).

In September 2002, the USDA held a simulated scenario of its own in which it was assumed that terrorists had introduced a foreign animal disease into the country. Though details of the scenario are being kept secret, concerns have arisen about interagency communication. "The biggest thing I learned is, 'I'm glad they're practicing,'" says AFIA's Bossman, who was invited to observe the exercise. Eighty agencies that don't normally communicate had to interact closely, he says. What Bossman also found "disconcerting" was that government agencies didn't involve industry in the planning process for the scenario simulation.

Containment can be facilitated not only by practice drills that try to anticipate a major event but also by some routine practices designed to head off the spread of any infectious diseases among herds. Commonsense measures can be taken even before a disease is identified, says Iowa State's Roth. For example, he notes that cattle are normally sold from one farmer to another at an auction where all cattle for sale are present. "That's a terrible biosecurity problem," he says, noting that one sick animal can then infect another entire farm.

Roth proposes the use of virtual sales, such as those held weekly over the Internet in 2003 by Superior Livestock Auction of Brush, Colorado, and Ft. Worth, Texas; another option is to send video via satellite. But he concedes that farmers like to touch their merchandise and examine it up close, and that many farmers will be reluctant to make purchases based on video viewing alone.

Also with disease containment in mind experts have been championing a national livestock identification system, with APHIS-VS in 2002 approving a national ID plan that was presented to it by more than 30 industry groups, including the AFBF. While eartags have long been used to surveil diseases in certain animals, says Ragan, the goal of the new effort is to make such surveillance much more widespread. Just as important as marking the animals is physically tracking them, and Ragan says that APHIS is looking at tracking databases it currently uses as well as evaluating various IT [information technology] systems for tracking animals and animal products. If a diseased pig is discovered, for example, authorities could use the system to determine where the pig has been and what other animals it has been in contact with. These at-risk animals could then be tested and treated.

One sick animal can . . . infect an . . . entire farm.

Miller says that without such a system, tracking an animal's peregrinations can take two weeks, by which time a disease may have spread widely. Miller says the goal is to track down all potentially infected animals within 48 hours. Funding is yet to be determined. Tracking devices cost money, bringing up the inevitable question of who will pay for it.

IDs raise interesting legal issues, points out Iowa State's Roth. A farmer in Idaho, for example, might fear liability in Ohio if, say, an outbreak of salmonella is traced back to his or her farm. But an ID system would benefit most farmers by identifying the parties truly at fault. And it might limit the larger economic costs if it helped authorities to track down the cause of the problem sooner.

Lab security

The USDA and state labs house a panoply of pathogens that would tempt any terrorist bent on agricultural devastation. Recognizing the increased threat to such facilities, recent USDA efforts have helped tighten security at these labs. Much of the 2001 supplemental appropriation to the USDA went toward this purpose, according to USDA's Horn. "The department has made excellent progress in terms of securing its own labs and pathogen libraries," he says.

For example, the Office of the Inspector General has spearheaded a process of audits to establish accountability in USDA labs, and risk assessments have been conducted on many labs. In addition, the department is establishing new criteria for access to federal laboratories and germplasm (genetic material) collections, Horn says. A centralized pathogen/germplasm database is being established to ensure accountability among both researchers and diagnosticians who use the collections, he says.

In addition, Ragan notes that the APHIS-VS Center for Veterinary Biologics in Ames, Iowa, has undergone a major security upgrade. In December, APHIS reported that the facility had installed a biometric security system, and experts are updating disaster preparedness plans for the facility.

In addition, effective in February 2003, the Department of Health and Human Services and the USDA have established complementary regulations governing the possession, use, and transfer of select biological agents and toxins "that could pose a threat to public, animal, and plant health and safety," according to a statement by the Centers for Disease Control and Prevention (CDC); biomedical centers, academic institutions, and commercial manufacturing sites must register with the CDC and APHIS if they possess any of these agents that threaten human health. Both regulations will have a 60-day public comment period beginning February 7, 2003.

A strike against the U.S. farm animal industry could cause massive economic disruption and fear. That scenario was once merely food for thought. But since 9-11, the prospect of an agroterror attack, while still remote, has increased sufficiently that government, academia, and industry now agree it is time to put some meat on their bare-bones security efforts.

6

Deficiencies in the Health Care System Threaten America's Ability to Respond to Bioterror

Katherine Eban

Katherine Eban is a Brooklyn-based investigative journalist. She writes about medicine and public health for numerous national magazines.

The federal government is establishing elaborate programs to protect the United States against bioterrorism. However, it is not addressing problems, such as a lack of staff and facilities and increases in the cost of malpractice insurance, that weaken the country's health care system to the point where it can barely handle normal activity, let alone a bioterror emergency. The influx of cash for national security contrasts sharply with cutbacks in federal and state funding for general public health. Mass programs such as the one aimed at smallpox vaccination are likely to strain health care resources even further. Ongoing health care crises in cities such as Las Vegas and Atlanta, as well as reactions to the terrorist attacks in late 2001, reveal dangerous flaws in the health care system and in government communication that must be addressed if the nation is to be truly protected against bioterror.

Just before the July 4 holiday in 2002, as National Guardsmen with sniffer dogs monitored the nation's bridges and airports, Jerome Hauer, an assistant secretary at the Health and Human Services Department, dispatched a technician to Atlanta to set up a satellite phone for the new director of the Centers for Disease Control (CDC).

If smallpox broke out, if phones failed, if the federal government had to oversee mass vaccination of an urban center, Hauer would have a way to communicate with the CDC director, who since fall 2001 has worked with him on health crises, particularly bioterror. It was one of many pre-

Katherine Eban, "Waiting for Bioterror," *The Nation*, vol. 275, December 9, 2002, p. 11. Copyright © 2002 by The Nation magazine/The Nation Company, Inc. Reproduced by permission.

cautions that might make the difference between a manageable event and full-scale disaster.

But at the same time, an attempt at crisis management of a more immediate kind was unfolding 2,500 miles to the west. As the FBI chased reports of potential new threats, including a possible attack on Las Vegas, Dr. John Fildes, the medical director of Nevada's only top-level trauma center, watched helplessly as a real medical disaster developed, one that had nothing and everything to do with the problems that Hauer was working to solve.

Faced with a dramatic spike in the cost of their malpractice insurance, fifty-seven of the fifty-eight orthopedic surgeons at University Medical Center in Las Vegas resigned, forcing the state's only trauma center that could treat it all—from car crash, burn and gunshot victims to potential bioterror casualties—to close for ten days.

This flurry of interest and concern [about bioterrorism] has not begun to address America's greatest public health vulnerability: the decrepit and deteriorating state of our healthcare system.

With Las Vegas a potential target, a quarter-million tourists at the gaming tables and the closest high-level trauma center 300 miles away, the crisis barely registered in the federal government. Nevada's Office of Emergency Management called to inquire about a backup plan, which, as Dr. Fildes later recounted, was to dissolve the county's trauma system, send patients to less prepared hospitals and take the critically injured to Los Angeles or Salt Lake City, both about eighty minutes by helicopter.

During that anxious week Hauer's satellite phone and Fildes's resignation letters formed two bookends of the nation's disaster planning. Hauer—whose Office of the Assistant Secretary for Public Health Emergency Preparedness (ASPHEP) was created by the department Secretary, Tommy Thompson, after the 2001 anthrax attacks—can get a last-minute satellite phone, a crack staff and even the ear of President Bush on public health concerns.

But Fildes, whose trauma center is the third-busiest in the nation and serves a 10,000-square-mile area, struggles to keep his staff intact and the doors of his center open. And this is in a state with no appointed health director, few mental health facilities, no extra room in its hospitals and the nation's only metropolitan area, Las Vegas, without a public health laboratory within 100 miles. In the event of a public health disaster, like a bioterror attack, Fildes says, "we're prepared to do our best. And I hope our best is good enough."

A public health "train wreck"

On taking office, President Bush eliminated the health position from the National Security Council, arguing that health, while in the national interest, was not a national security concern. In the wake of the anthrax attacks, he changed his tune, declaring, "We have fought the causes and consequences of disease throughout history and must continue to do so with every available means." The 2003 budget for biodefense is up 319 percent, to $5.9 billion. States, newly flush with $1.1 billion in biodefense funds, have gone on shopping sprees for emergency equipment like gas masks, hazmat suits and Geiger counters. Newly drafted to fight the war on bioterror, doctors and public health officials are now deemed vital to national security, and their hospitals are even under threat, according to an alert released in mid-November 2002 by the Federal Bureau of Investigation (FBI).

And yet this flurry of interest and concern has not begun to address America's greatest public health vulnerability: the decrepit and deteriorating state of our healthcare system. In states from Nevada to Georgia, dozens of health officials and doctors told *The Nation* that anemic state funding, overcrowding and staff shortages may be greater problems in responding to bioterror than lack of equipment or specific training. "We don't have enough ER capacity in this country to get through tonight's 911 calls," said Dr. Arthur Kellerman, chairman of the emergency medicine department at the Emory University School of Medicine in Atlanta. Two decades of managed care and government cuts have left a depleted system with too few hospitals, overburdened staff, declining access for patients, rising emergency-room visits and an increasing number of uninsured. The resulting strain is practically Kafkaesque: How do you find enough nurses to staff enough hospital beds to move enough emergency-room patients upstairs so that ambulances with new patients can stop circling the block?

The solution, say doctors, is to tackle the systemic and not just the boutique problems.

The infusion of cash for bioterror defense without consideration of these fundamental problems is like "building walls in a bog," where they are sure to sink, said Dr. Jeffrey Koplan, the recently departed head of the CDC. Between 1980 and 2000, the number of hospitals declined by 900 because of declining payments and increased demands for efficiency, according to the American Hospital Association, leaving almost four-fifths of urban hospitals experiencing serious emergency-room overcrowding. Burnout and low pay have left 15 percent of the nation's nursing jobs unfilled, and the staffing shortage has led to a drop in the number of hospital beds by one-fifth; in Boston by one-third, according to the Center for Studying Health System Change in Washington.

Meanwhile, emergency-room visits increased by 5 million in 2001, according to the American College of Emergency Physicians. One in eight urban hospitals diverts or turns away new emergency patients one-fifth of the time because of overcrowding, the American Hospital Association reports. And the costs of health insurance and medical malpractice premiums continue to soar.

In public health, chronic underfunding has closed training programs and depleted expertise. According to a recent CDC report, 78 percent of the nation's public health officials lack advanced training and more than half have no basic health training at all. During the anthrax crisis inex-

ST CHARLES COMMUNITY COLLEGE
LIBRARY
WITHDRAWN

perienced technicians in the New York City public health laboratory failed to turn on an exhaust fan while testing anthrax samples and accidentally contaminated the laboratory.

A government study of rural preparedness in April 2002 found that only 20 percent of the nation's 3,000 local public health departments have a plan in place to respond to bioterror. Thirteen states have had no epidemiologists on payroll, said Dr. Elin Gursky, senior fellow for biodefense and public health programs at the ANSER (Analytic Services, Inc.) Institute for Homeland Security. Meanwhile, 18 percent of jobs in the nation's public health labs are open, and the salaries create little hope of filling them. One state posted the starting salary for the director of its public health laboratory program—a Ph.D. position—at $38,500, said Scott Becker, executive director of the Association of Public Health Laboratories. Becker calls the combination of state cuts and work-force shortages a "train wreck."

Amid this crisis, clinicians have a new mandate: to be able to fight a war on two fronts simultaneously. They must care for the normal volume of patients and track the usual infectious diseases while being able to treat mass casualties of a terrorist event. They now have some money for the high-concept disaster, but with many states in dire financial straits, there is less money than ever for the slow-motion meltdown of the healthcare system, in which 41 million Americans lack health insurance. In the event of a smallpox attack, the tendency of the uninsured to delay seeking treatment could be catastrophic.

Hauer hopes that the "dual use" of federal resources could herald a golden age in public health, with tools for tracking anthrax or smallpox being used also to combat West Nile virus or outbreaks from contaminated food. But politicians of all stripes continue to propose beefing up biodefense in isolation from more systemic problems. In October 2002, Al Gore argued in a speech that the problem of the uninsured should take "a back seat" temporarily to the more urgent matter of biodefense. And Bush has proposed shifting key public health and biodefense functions into his proposed Department of Homeland Security, a move likely to weaken daily public health work like disease surveillance and prevention, according to the General Accounting Office. A bipartisan report issued by the Council on Foreign Relations in 2002 warned that America remains dangerously unprepared for a terrorist attack, with its emergency responders untrained and its public health systems depleted.

"Every hospital bed in this county is full every day."

The solution, say doctors, is to tackle the systemic and not just the boutique problems. "If you have a health system that is chaotic and has no leadership and is not worried about tuberculosis and West Nile and just worried about these rare entities, you'll never be prepared," said Dr. Lewis Goldfrank, director of emergency medicine at Bellevue Hospital Center in New York City. "To be useful, money has to be earmarked for public health generally, so that it will prepare you for terrorism or naturally occurring events."

President Bush strongly resisted federalizing airport security until it became clear as day that private security companies and their minimum-wage workers would continue to let a flow of box cutters, knives and handguns through the metal detectors. Some clinicians now say that the specter of bioterror raises a similar question, which almost nobody in Washington has yet begun to address: Has healthcare become so vital to national security that it must be centralized, with the federal government guaranteeing basic healthcare for everyone?

"Forget about paying for the smallpox vaccine," said Dr. Carlos del Rio, chief of medicine at Atlanta's Grady Memorial Hospital. "Who's going to pay for the complications of the vaccine? With what money? We haven't even addressed that. As you look at bioterror issues, it's forcing us to look at our healthcare delivery."

Crisis management in crisis

Hauer spends much of his time in a windowless set of offices within the vast Health and Human Services Department, trouble-shooting the medical consequences of a hypothetical dirty bomb or intentional smallpox outbreak. He must also navigate the knotted bureaucracy of forty federal agencies that respond to terrorism, twenty of which play some role in bioterror response, and guide the states through infrastructure problems so severe they boggle the mind. His tactic at a meeting in Washington in August 2002 with state emergency managers was to put the fear of God into them. In the event of mass vaccinations for smallpox, the logistics are "very daunting," he told the small and sleepy group in a conference room at the Mayflower Hotel. "They will fall on emergency management, and the health departments will turn to you and say, 'You need to open 200 vaccination centers.'"

This seemed to focus the group. Before Hauer got up, these local and regional representatives had been talking about lessons learned from managing hurricanes and the best kinds of hand-held chemical-weapons detectors.

Tommy Thompson created Hauer's office after the CDC, then his lead agency on bioterror, appeared to bungle the anthrax response and the Administration found itself in a scientific and logistical quagmire. Some officials claimed the White House muzzled the CDC. Others accused the CDC of sloth and bad science for failing to realize quickly that anthrax spores can leak from taped envelopes. Hauer seemed like a good choice to find a way out of this mess: He had developed the nation's first bioterrorism response plan as director of New York City's Office of Emergency Management under Mayor Rudolph Giuliani.

Hauer told the group that his office had moved $1.1 billion to the states in ninety days and was now doing audits, offering technical assistance and helping to stage drills.

But it was the nitty-gritty of mass vaccination that really quieted the room. Training a vaccinator usually takes two hours, though it can be done in fifteen minutes; for every million people vaccinated, about two will die; the vaccinators need to be federally insured because of liability; and all those vaccinated must keep the vaccination site unexposed to others for up to twenty-one days. Who would pay the salaries of contract workers on their days off?

Few emergency managers seemed to have considered such problems. Most were still immersed in completing disaster plans and state budget battles, coping with teetering local health departments and vendors hawking "equipment that will detect the landing of Martians ten miles away in a windstorm," as James O'Brien, emergency manager for Clark County, Nevada, put it.

Hauer returned that afternoon to just such a morass: figuring out how to create a unified command for the national capital area, encompassing Maryland, Virginia and the District of Columbia, seventeen jurisdictions over 3,000 square miles, with embassies, consulates, the World Bank and the International Monetary Fund. He had assigned this problem to a team from the Office of Emergency Response (OER), the federal office under ASPHEP that coordinates medical resources during disasters, who arrived at his office to report their progress.

Each state, unsurprisingly, wanted to be the lead responder, and the team recommended that Hauer try to break the logjam and give direction. He pored over the list of those invited to a coordinating committee meeting—twenty-nine people from twenty-nine different agencies—and concluded, "We need to come away with plans, not some loosie-goosie love fest where everyone pats each other on the back and jerks each other off."

The OER team trooped out with its marching orders and the next meeting began. The CEO of the New York Blood Center, Dr. Robert Jones, with a DC consultant in tow, came to ask for money to expand the center's program of making umbilical cord (placental) blood, used for patients exposed to massive radiation. Jones said the center already had about 18,000 units of cord blood stored in "bioarchive freezers" on First Avenue in Manhattan.

"You might want to think about storing it away from Manhattan," said Hauer, suggesting the obvious, as he got out a little booklet and looked up a one-kiloton nuclear bomb. "You'd need 20,000 to 40,000 units" to begin treating a city of people, said Hauer. "What's the lead time for getting it into a patient?"

Jones, who had never met Hauer before, seemed surprised to be taken so seriously and to be crunching numbers about three minutes into the conversation. Hauer, wanting to stockpile cord blood, seemed surprised that Jones had not brought a written proposal with a dollar amount. This was no time to be coy about asking for money.

Suddenly Hauer's secure phone rang and the room fell silent. "This is Jerry Hauer," he said. "You have the wrong number."

Leaving Las Vegas—in the lurch

In Las Vegas, a gaming town with an appetite for risk, little by way of a medical infrastructure ever developed. With the population exploding and 6,000 families a month moving into the Las Vegas area in Clark County, population 1.4 million, it is also dramatically short on hospitals. By a thumbnail calculation—for every 100,000 people you need 200 beds—the county, which has eleven hospitals, is 600 beds short, said Dr. John Ellerton, chief of staff at University Medical Center, where the trauma center closed.

Even if you build more hospitals, how would you staff them? The state ranks fiftieth in its nurse-to-patient ratio, and because of the malpractice crisis, ninety of the state's 2,000 doctors have closed their practices and another eighty-three said they have considered leaving, according to Lawrence Matheis, executive director of the Nevada State Medical Association. The overcrowded emergency rooms are closed to new patients 40 percent of the time. Paramedics often drive and drive, waiting for an open emergency room. In turn, patients can wait four hours for an X-ray, three for a lab test. "There is no surge capacity, minimal staffing, minimal equipment," said Dr. Donald Kwalick, chief health officer of Clark County. "Every hospital bed in this county is full every day."

At times, the populace and even the doctors have seemed strangely indifferent. One night in the summer of 2000 an ambulance crew from the private company American Medical Response got called to a casino, and as they wheeled a stretcher amid the gaming tables, not a single patron looked up. Their patient: a man with a possible heart attack slumped over a slot machine. "The purity of our devotion to individual liberties tends to diminish our security and humane concern," said Matheis.

"Try not to get sick between 5 P.M. and midnight."

The September 11, 2001, attacks did not entirely transform this mindset. Since 1998 the city had been included on a federal government list of 120 cities that should prepare for possible attack. Eleven of the world's thirteen largest hotels, ones with more than 5,000 rooms, are here. But in August 2002, even the president of the state's medical association, Dr. Robert Schreck, said he worried little about terrorism. Al Qaeda's intent is "to kill capitalism," he said, sipping wine in the lobby of the elaborate Venetian Hotel, home to a massive casino and dozens of stores. "Why would they hit us?"

But in 2001 Nevadans began to lose their cool as the medical system disintegrated. As malpractice insurance premiums skyrocketed, about thirty of Clark County's ninety-three obstetricians closed down their practices. Insurers, trying to reduce risk by limiting the remaining obstetricians to 125 deliveries a year, left thousands of pregnant women to hunt for doctors, some by desperately rifling through the Yellow Pages under "D." In 2002, the last pediatric cardiac surgery practice packed up and left the state.

Not surprisingly, Nevada was also unprepared for the anthrax crisis. In October 2001, when Microsoft's Reno office got suspicious powder in the mail that initially tested positive, an "outbreak of hysteria" ensued, said Matheis. The Clark County health district got 1,200 phone calls reporting everything from sugar to chalk dust, and investigated 500 of them with its skeletal staff. The state had no stockpiled antibiotics, and without a lab in Clark County, samples were shipped 500 miles north to Reno for testing.

The new federal money for bioterror preparedness, $10.5 million for Nevada alone, will help enormously. Of that, more than $2 million will go to building a public health laboratory in Las Vegas. But the money will do nothing to solve the problems of staff shortages and soaring medical malpractice premiums that forced the trauma center to close in July.

By July 4, the city of Las Vegas awoke to maximum fear of terror and a minimal medical system, with the trauma center closed for a second day. Governor Kenny Guinn had called an emergency session of the legislature and vowed to make sure that doctors did not abandon the state. An official at the nearby Nellis Air Force Base called the chief of orthopedics, Dr. Anthony Serfustini, asking what to do in the event of injuries. The lanky surgeon said that he reminded the man, You're the Air Force. You can fly your pilots to San Bernardino.

The community's medical infrastructure had declined to a level not seen in twenty-five years, said Dr. Fildes. And on July 4, the inevitable happened. Jim Lawson, 59, a grandfather of nine, was extracted from his mangled car and rushed to a nearby hospital—one with a nervous staff and little up-to-date trauma training—and died about an hour later. His daughter, Mary Rasar, said that she believes the trauma center, had it been open, could have saved him.

Atlanta's health emergency

On September 11, 2001, Dr. Arthur Kellerman was in Washington waiting to testify before Congress about the consequences of uninsurance when a plane struck the Pentagon, across the street from his hotel room. He immediately called back to Grady Memorial Hospital in Atlanta, where he oversees the emergency room residents, and got a disturbing report.

While Atlanta appeared to be safe from terrorism, the emergency room had twenty-five admitted patients waiting for hospital beds, the intensive-care area was packed and the staff had shut the emergency room to new patients. Worse, every emergency room in central Atlanta had declared saturation at the same time. None were taking new patients, and loaded ambulances were circling the block. If attacks had occurred in Atlanta that morning, "there was no way on God's earth we could have absorbed more patients," said Kellerman. Since then, all the Atlanta-area hospitals have gone on simultaneous diversion numerous times, leaving "nowhere to put casualties."

For three weeks, from the initial [anthrax] outbreak on October 4, 2002, Americans seeking clear information from the CDC were out of luck.

Despite all the effort to gear up for biological terror, the problem of overcrowded and understaffed emergency rooms—where terror's victims would be treated—has received only spotty attention. *U.S. News & World Report* featured the problem as a cover story, "Code Blue: Crisis in the E.R.," but it ran on September 10, 2001. A month after the attacks, Representative Henry Waxman prepared a report on ambulance diversions and their effect on disaster preparedness, finding a problem in thirty-two states. In at least nine states, every hospital in a local area had diverted ambulances simultaneously on a number of occasions, causing harm or even death to some patients. In Atlanta, one diverted patient was admitted only after he slipped into respiratory arrest while in the idling ambulance. The report quoted an editorial from the *St. Louis Post-Dispatch* last year:

> A word to the wise: Try not to get sick between 5 P.M. and midnight, when hospitals are most likely to go on diversion. Try not to get sick or injured at all in St. Louis or Kansas City, where diversions are most frequent. And if you're unlucky enough to end up in the back of an ambulance diverted from one E.R. to another, use the extra time to pray.

In Washington, Hauer has directed each region to identify 500 extra beds that can be "surged" or put into use quickly, which has led a number of states to identify armories, school auditoriums, stadiums and hotels that can be used as MASH hospitals. But no bubble tent can replace a hospital bed, with a full complement of services readily available within the "golden hour" so crucial to treating trauma patients, said Kellerman. And no proposal exists to address the problem as a systemic one, in which a shortage of nurses and cutbacks in reimbursement have made it impossible for hospitals to staff enough beds.

Without a solution in sight, Grady Memorial uses a makeshift system, parking admitted patients on stretchers in the hallways beneath handwritten numbers that run from 1 to 30. With the crisis deepening, more numbers—1a, 1b, 1c, for example, seventeen additional spaces in all—have been squeezed between the initial numbers up and down the hall. The other night Kellerman had fifty patients lined up waiting for rooms. "These are not disaster scenarios," he said. "This is Friday night. Wednesday afternoon."

September 11's hard lessons

New York City, with sixty-four hospitals, more than any other in the country, was probably the best prepared for a mass-casualty incident. Except that on September 11, most of the victims were dead. Within minutes, the Bellevue emergency room was crowded with hundreds of doctors, each bed with its own team of specialists, from surgeons and psychiatrists to gynecologists. "The entire physician and nursing force of the hospital just came down at once," said Dr. Brian Wexler, a third-year emergency medicine resident. At Long Island College Hospital in Brooklyn, Dr. Lewis Kohl, chairman of emergency medicine, said that by noon, he had a doctor and a nurse for each available bed and could have tripled that number. Doctors from all over the country at a defibrillation conference in downtown Brooklyn were begging to work. "I spent most of the day sending volunteers away," he recalled.

Tragically, so many people died that doctors had little to do. But the people who answered phones, counseled the distraught or drew blood from volunteers were overrun. A web-based patient locator system cobbled together by the Greater New York Hospital Association got 2 million hits within days from frantic relatives. Beth Israel Medical Center ran out of social workers, psychologists and psychiatrists to answer calls. "I answered the phone for half an hour and said, 'I'm not qualified to do this,'" said Lisa Hogarty, vice president of facility management for Continuum Health Partners, which runs Beth Israel.

If anything, New York learned that targeted improvements, such as the creation of regional bioterror treatment centers, will not work. Susan Waltman, senior vice president of the Greater New York Hospital Association, told a CDC advisory committee in June 2002 that on September 11, 7,200 people, many covered in debris, wound up at 100 different hospitals, jumping on trains, boats and subways, or walking, to get away from downtown Manhattan. Now imagine if the debris had been tainted with some infectious biological agent. "You can't put the concentration of knowledge or staffing or supplies in regional centers," she said, "because you can't control where patients go."

The anthrax attacks, when they came, were a wake-up call of the worst kind. Baffled government officials with minimal scientific knowledge attributed the outbreak initially to farm visits, then contaminated water and finally to a fine, weaponized anthrax that had been sent through the mail. With no clear chain of communication or command for testing the samples, reporting the results, advising the medical community or informing the public, samples vanished into dozens of laboratories. Conference calls between officials from different local, state and federal agencies were required to track them down, said those involved with the investigation. Testing methods were not standardized, with the Environmental Protection Agency, the postal service, the CDC, the FBI and the Defense Department all swabbing desktops and mailrooms using different methods and different kits, some of which had never been evaluated before. "A lot of those specimens that were said to be positive were not," said Dr. Philip Brachman, an anthrax expert and professor at the Rollins School of Public Health at Emory University.

For three weeks, from the initial outbreak on October 4, 2001, Americans seeking clear information from the CDC were out of luck. Until October 20, the agency's website still featured diabetes awareness month instead of the anthrax attacks. Dr. David Fleming, the CDC's deputy director for science and public health, said that while the CDC did respond quickly and accurately, "we were too focused on getting the public health job done, and we were not proactive in getting our message out."

But it wasn't just the CDC. Few officials nationwide knew what to do. In New York, police were marching into the city's public health laboratory carrying furniture and computers they suspected of being tainted, recalled Dr. David Perlin, scientific director of the Public Health Research Institute, an advanced microbiology center then located a few floors above the city lab. Since those terrible days, the CDC under new director Dr. Julie Gerberding has made a great effort to establish its leadership and develop emergency response systems. "We have the people, we have the plans and now we have the practice," Gerberding, a microbiologist and veteran of the anthrax investigation, declared on September 11, 2002. "We're building our knowledge and capacity every day to assure that CDC and our partners are ready to respond to any terrorist event."

After September 11, however, such confident talk rings a little hollow. In September 2002 the CDC laid out a radical plan for vaccinating much of the country within a week in the event of a smallpox attack. Medical experts greeted the plan as unrealistic and almost impossible to execute, given that disasters inevitably depart from plans to address them. They are pressing for the prevaccination of critical healthcare workers, and a decision on this is soon to be announced [such a program began later in December 2002].

Preparing for the worst

Past a strip mall outside Washington, and down a nondescript road, the federal Office of Emergency Preparedness (OEP) keeps a warehouse of equipment that can all but navigate the end of civilization. It has the world's most sophisticated portable morgue units, each one able to support numerous autopsies. Another pile of boxes unfolds to become a full operating theater that can support open-heart surgery, if need be.

All this equipment can function during "catastrophic infrastructure failure," said Gary Moore, deputy director of the agency. And all of it can be loaded onto a C-5 transport plane and flown anywhere in the world. The federal government has massive resources—twelve fifty-ton pallets of drugs called the National Pharmaceutical Stockpile, which can get anywhere in the country in seven to twelve hours. After the New York City laboratory became contaminated, the Defense Department flew in six tons of laboratory equipment and turned a two-person testing operation into ten laboratories with three evidence rooms, a command center and seventy-five lab technicians operating around the clock.

This monumental surge capacity is crucial to preparedness. So are supplies. Dr. Kohl at Long Island College Hospital, who describes himself as a "paranoid of very long standing," feels ready. He's got a padlocked room full of gas masks, Geiger counters and Tyvek suits of varying thicknesses, most purchased after the anthrax attacks. Pulling one off the shelf, he declared confidently, "You could put this on and hang out in a bucket of Sarin [a nerve poison used in chemical attacks]."

But none of this can replace the simple stuff: hospital beds, trained people, fax machines, an infrastructure adequate for everyday use. Indeed, as states slash their public health and medical budgets, the opposite may be happening: We are building high-tech defenses on an ever-weakening infrastructure. In Colorado, for example, Governor Bill Owens cut all state funding for local public health departments in part because the federal government was supplying new funds. Public health officials there suddenly have federal money to hire bioterror experts but not enough state money to keep their offices open. While the Larimer County health department got $100,000 in targeted federal money, it lost $700,000 in state funds and fifteen staff positions. A spokesman for Governor Owens did not return calls seeking comment. States across the country are making similar cuts, said Dr. Gursky of the ANSER Institute, their weakened staffs left to prepare for bioterror while everyday health threats continue unchecked.

From her office window, Dr. Ruth Berkelman, director of Emory's Center for Public Health Preparedness, can see the new, $193 million infectious-disease laboratory rising on the CDC's forty-six-acre campus. While the new laboratory and information systems are needed, she says, if we detect smallpox, it's going to be because some doctor in an emergency room gets worried and "picks up the telephone."

7

The American Health Care System's Preparedness for Bioterror Has Improved

American Public Health Association

The American Public Health Association is the oldest and largest organization of public health professionals in the world, including researchers, administrators, health service providers, and teachers.

Since the terrorist attacks of September 11, 2001, the United States has done little to deal with underlying problems that contribute to terrorism, such as poverty, human rights abuses, and disparities in health care. However, it has strengthened the public health infrastructure in ways that improve its ability to respond to terror attacks and has increased the supply of medicines and vaccines that would be available after an attack. It has somewhat improved the education of health professionals and the public about terrorism and taken steps to address the mental health needs of populations affected by terrorism. It has made the food and water supply more secure, and data collection systems have been improved.

T he American Public Health Association developed its Guiding Principles for a Public Health Response to Terrorism soon after the attacks of September 11, 2001. This report card assesses whether U.S. policy since the attacks has been consistent with these principles. We can and should strive to always improve and evaluate our preparedness for a terrorist attack. For decades, public health has been grossly underfunded. Since Sept. 11, new investments in our nation's public health system have begun to reverse this trend and better prepare the public health system in the event of an attack. It is critical that such investments are sustained. It is also important that funding for bioterrorism preparedness does not supplant resources needed for other important public health activities. This "report card" analysis examines the progress we have made to improve our public health readiness and highlights areas in need of additional attention.

American Public Health Association, "One Year After the Terrorist Attacks: Is Public Health Prepared? A Report Card from the American Public Health Association," www.apha.org, Fall 2002. Copyright © 2002 by American Public Health Association. Reproduced by permission.

1 Address poverty, social injustice and health disparities that may contribute to the development of terrorism. D

– In 2002, the U.S. Budget for foreign development, humanitarian and economic aid, as a proportion of the overall budget, is at its lowest level since the end of World War II.

– At the end of 2001, 40 million adults and children were infected with HIV/AIDS. The United States is the richest country in the world, but of the G8 countries [a group of major industrial democracies that includes France, the United States, Britain, Germany, Japan, Italy, Canada, and Russia], it has contributed one of the lowest amounts to the new Global Fund For AIDS, TB [tuberculosis] and Malaria as a proportion of its overall wealth. A Central Intelligence Agency (CIA) report concluded that the "persistent infectious disease burden is likely to aggravate and, in some cases, may even provoke economic decay, social fragmentation and political destabilization in the hardest hit countries in the developing and former communist worlds."

+ On July 18, 2002, the full Senate Appropriations Committee approved their version of the Fiscal Year (FY) 2003 Foreign Operations bill. Overall, the bill includes $16.4 billion, which is a $953 million increase above FY 2002's levels for foreign assistance programs. The bill includes small funding increases for HIV/AIDS, child and maternal health, family planning programs and infectious disease control.

2 Provide humanitarian assistance to, and protect the human rights of, the civilian populations of all nations that are directly or indirectly affected by terrorism. C

+ Human rights violations such as discrimination or violence against women and children and harmful traditional practices can have serious health consequences. In 2002, for the first time, the Commission on Human Rights, the main United Nations (U.N.) policy-making body on human rights, adopted a resolution on the right to health to appoint a special rapporteur (an independent expert) to report annually to the Commission on the extent to which governments are fulfilling the right to health.

+ U.N. member states voted to explore the creation of a new mechanism within the International Covenant on Economic, Social and Cultural Rights whereby individuals can petition their governments at the international level for failure to respect, protect or fulfill the right to health and other economic and social rights.

– The Administration proposes a minimal increase in spending for International Development and Humanitarian Assistance and for the Economic Support fund from a total of $11.5 billion in FY2002 to $11.6 billion in 2003. These initiatives were level funded in 2002. The President's proposal for a Millennium Challenge account does not call for any increases in foreign economic aid until 2004.

– The United States identified the restoration of Afghan women's basic rights as one of the principal goals of ousting the Taliban. After the Sept. 11 attacks, the U.S. government threw its full energies into combating terrorism emerging from militants in the Islamic world. But it has done little to expose and condemn the ways some states are using radical interpretations of Islamic law, or Shariah, to subordinate and exclude women.

3 Advocate the speedy end of the armed conflict in Afghanistan and promote non-violent means of conflict resolution. B+
+ Afghanistan has been mired in conflict for over 20 years. The U.S. military campaign began on Oct. 7, 2001, against the Taliban movement that ruled the country and hosted the Al Qaeda terrorist organization. The Taliban collapsed at the hands of the U.S. and Afghan opposition military in November–December 2001. Although the military campaign is largely over, U.S. forces remain in Afghanistan in late 2002, serving as peacekeepers and searching for Taliban and Al Qaeda fighters and leaders that remain at large.

+ In June 2002 Hamid Karzai was confirmed by an Emergency Loya Jirga (grand council) as head of a Transitional Administration.

+ The United States is working to further stabilize an interim government, arrange humanitarian and reconstruction assistance and expand the Afghan national army in order to maintain stability.

+ The United Nations and the United States are in the process of lifting U.N. and international sanctions imposed on Afghanistan since the Soviet occupation.

State and local governments will receive $1.1 billion to create bioterrorism surveillance programs.

---

4 Strengthen the public health infrastructure (which includes workforce, laboratory and information systems) and other components of the public health system (including education, research and the faith community) to increase the ability to identify, respond to, and prevent the problems of public health importance, including the health aspects of terrorist attacks. B
+ Comprehensive state plans to strengthen public health systems and prepare for terrorist attacks were approved by the U.S. Department of Health and Human Services (HHS) in June 2002. State and local governments will receive $1.1 billion to create bioterrorism surveillance programs, improve infectious disease surveillance and enable hospitals to deal with large numbers of casualties. The funds are being used to renovate laboratories and increase their capacity, improve the detection of bioterrorism and other infectious disease outbreaks, train health workers, improve bioterrorism response facilities and equipment and develop surge capacity, and ensure that at least 500 hospital beds are available in each community to handle a sudden influx of bioterrorism victims.

+ On May 12, 2002, The Bioterrorism Preparedness Act was signed into law. The law aims to address gaps in biodefense, surveillance systems and public health infrastructure through federal investment in research, planning and preparedness.

+ The Centers for Disease Control and Prevention (CDC) has created diagnostic and epidemiological guidelines for state and local health departments and will be assisting states in holding drills to assess bioterrorism preparedness.

+ Since Sept. 11, the CDC has funded the development of new laboratories throughout the country that can test for microbes and chemicals that might be involved in a bioterrorist attack. There is at least one such laboratory in each state.

+ As of July 23, 2002, 17 states have introduced legislation based, in whole or in part, on a model State Emergency Health Powers law. This model was developed by the Center for Law and Public Health at Georgetown and Johns Hopkins Universities. The model law recognizes that governors and public health authorities may need additional temporary authority to respond rapidly and effectively in the case of an emergency in order to protect the public's health. CDC believes that almost all states have used the draft model law as an assessment tool in reviewing their public health statutes.

– There currently does not exist a baseline set of performance goals and measures upon which to assess and improve preparedness. Without such national outcome measures in place to ensure that the states and localities use federal money for the purpose for which they are intended, we risk a divergence of priorities between the federal, state and local governments. This may result in state and local governments supplanting their own previous levels of commitment in these areas with new federal resources.

– Coordination at a regional level is still lacking. Preparation in rural areas falls behind the level of preparedness in major metropolitan areas.

New technology is allowing for quicker checks of food.

---

5 *Ensure availability of, and accessibility to, health care, including medications and vaccines, for individuals exposed, infected, made ill, or injured in terrorist attacks. B+*

+ Since Sept. 11, 2001, the National Pharmaceutical Stockpile Program managed by the CDC has stockpiled enough smallpox vaccines to vaccinate the entire U.S. population. In addition, HHS will have enough of the anthrax antibiotic cipro stockpiled by the end of 2002 to treat 20 million people.

+ HHS has also increased from eight to 12 the number of "push packs" that are stockpiled. Each Push Pack has at least 84 different types of supplies, such as antibiotics, needles and nerve-gas antidotes. These 12 stockpiles, located throughout the United States, can be available anywhere in the country within 12 hours.

+ The National Health Service Corps plans to recruit 40 new U.S. Public Health Service officers to work in medically underserved communities. In addition to providing primary health care services, the officers will be available to respond to local or national emergencies.

+ In July 2002, HHS made $2 million in grants available to develop volunteer Medical Reserve Corps units on the local level. The grants will be used to train volunteers to assist medical professionals during large-scale emergencies to be transported to the site of a bioterrorist event within 12 hours.

+ The National Disaster Medical System now has over 10,000 volunteer healthcare workers that can deploy within hours to the scene of an attack.

– There currently exists a severe shortage of epidemiologists, microbiologists and public health nurses. Although $20 million has been funneled to training programs in public health schools, it is going to take time to educate and train these important public health professionals.

– Despite new funding approved for hospital preparedness, most of the money has yet to reach institutions in need. In April 2002, 78 percent of hospitals indicated that a shortage of funds is keeping them from creating systems to track and identify outbreaks, train personnel and improve communications capabilities. Hospitals have voiced major concerns about the current lack of "surge capacity," the ability of hospitals to accommodate a sudden increase of patients.

6 Educate and inform health professionals and the public to better identify, respond to, and prevent the health consequences of terrorism, and promote the visibility and availability of health professionals in the communities they serve. B

+ Many medical schools and teaching hospitals held special programs on emergency preparedness and anthrax exposure following Sept. 11. Many schools have revised the contents of courses on infectious diseases and pathological physiology to include information related to bioterrorism.

– There is no general consensus as to how medical schools should address bioterrorism preparedness in their curricula.

+ The Web site of the CDC provides detailed information for health professionals and the public on biological and chemical agents and gives instructions on what to do in case of a biological or chemical attack.

– According to the Association of Public Health Laboratories, a shortage of qualified laboratory professionals remains.

7 Address the mental health needs of populations directly or indirectly affected by terrorism. B

+ The National Institute of Mental Health (NIMH) responded to the Sept. 11 terrorist attacks by awarding new grants for research on mental health needs. The grants were funded through its Rapid Assessment Post Impact of Disaster (RAPID) grants program, and are aimed at helping to design large-scale studies on prevention and treatment of mental illnesses resulting from exposure to mass violence.

+ The Public Health Security and Bioterrorism Preparedness and Response Act was signed into law on June 12, 2002. It allocates $1.6 billion in grants to help states improve bioterrorism and mental health disaster response. A portion of that money would fund more counseling and training in disaster response.

– Teams of counselors and therapists are still needed and being trained to help the public cope with possible future catastrophe. Efforts are being made but according to Dr. Ann Norwood, chairwoman of the American Psychiatric Association's committee on disasters, they are not quite there.

+ The military announced in August 2002 that U.S. soldiers will be screened for psychological problems before they leave Afghanistan and commanders will watch out for symptoms of depression and anxiety among their troops.

8 Ensure the protection of the environment, the food and water supply, and the health and safety of rescue and recovery workers. B

+ All U.S. water authorities have begun vulnerability assessments since

Sept. 11. The largest plants will finish their assessments by December 2002, and the smaller plants should be finished by December 2003. In addition, most plants have significantly tightened security by ending tours, installing new security systems and screening drivers.

– Thousands of facilities, including chemical plants and water treatment plants, use and store hazardous chemicals in quantities that put millions of Americans at risk in the event of a release.

+ The U.S. Environmental Protection Agency (EPA) received a supplemental appropriation from Congress of $89 million to improve safety and security of the nation's water supply. The EPA's Water Protection Task Force and Regional Offices, working with many partners, are taking actions to improve the security of the nation's drinking water by providing direct grant assistance to drinking water facilities, supporting the development of tools and technical assistance to small and medium drinking and wastewater utilities, and promoting information sharing and research to improve treatment and detection methods.

+ In 2001 the number of food inspectors was 125. In 2002 Congress provided the funds to hire up to 750 new inspectors.

+ New technology is allowing for quicker checks of food.

– HHS Secretary Tommy Thompson recently singled out food inspections as an area of particular concern and vulnerability. Experts are concerned that gaps in biological and intelligence data on foreign-plant and foreign-animal pest and pathogens and inadequate inspections at the nation's borders increase the threat to the nation's food supply.

Operation TIPS . . . seems to propose that the government recruit informants among letter carriers and utility workers.

---

9 Assure clarification of the roles, relationships and responsibilities among public health agencies, law enforcement and first responders. C

+ The proposed Department of Homeland Security, if enacted, will have a central role in coordinating and consolidating preparedness efforts. [The department was created.]

+ In late 2002, the Federal Response Plan gives the Federal Bureau of Investigation the authority to coordinate law enforcement efforts following an act of terrorism, while the Federal Emergency Management Agency (FEMA) is responsible for coordinating measures to protect the public health and safety. In the event of an act of chemical/biological terrorism, HHS will work with FEMA to perform hazard detection, threat assessment, decontamination and medical support tasks.

– The General Accounting Office concluded that a highly integrated approach to the homeland security effort has not yet been achieved.

– The roles of state and local agencies and first responders are not clearly defined. According to the Federal Response Plan, in the event of a terrorist attack "Local, State and Federal Responders will define working perimeters that may overlap. . . . Control of these perimeters may be enforced by different authorities, which will impede the overall response if adequate coordination is not established."

– A significant barrier to services exists due to inflexible physician licensure requirements during the case of an emergency. Physicians currently are not permitted to practice outside the state in which they are licensed. This limits coordination on a regional or intrastate level in the case of a public health emergency. Legislation is needed to establish an advance registration system for physician volunteers, which verifies their credentials, licenses and hospital privileges.

10 Prevent hate crimes, ethnic, racial and religious discrimination, including profiling; promote cultural competence, diversity training, and dialogue among peoples; and protect human rights and civil liberties. F
– Operation TIPS (Terrorism Information and Prevention System) was introduced as a Department of Justice program in development in January 2002. While few details are available about the program, it seems to propose that the government recruit informants among letter carriers and utility workers—people who enter the homes of Americans for reasons unrelated to law enforcement—to help conduct surveillance efforts. This could be a direct violation of civil rights and deserves closer scrutiny.

– In October 2001, Congress passed the Patriot Act, whose provisions included new government powers to detain foreign nationals suspected of involvement in terrorism or "any other activity that endangers the national security of the United States" for up to seven days without charge. The act authorizes the attorney general to continue to detain indefinitely on national security grounds foreign nationals charged with immigration violations, whose removal was "unlikely in the reasonably foreseeable future."

– The detentions of U.S. citizens Yaser Hamdi and Jose Padilla as "enemy combatants" may violate a 1971 law that bars citizens from being imprisoned or detained except pursuant to an act of Congress.

– In November 2001 President Bush signed a military order allowing for non–U.S. citizens suspected of involvement in "international terrorism" to be tried by special military commissions which would expressly bypass the normal rules of evidence and safeguards prevailing in the U.S. criminal justice system. Under the order, the commissions could operate in secret and pass death sentences, and their decisions could not be appealed to a higher court. Trials before such courts would violate the principle of non-discrimination and international fair trial standards.

– Secret deportation proceedings against aliens detained in terrorism investigations threaten basic civil rights. A total of 74 detainees remain in custody out of an estimated 1,200 that were rounded up after Sept. 11. Some were initially denied the right to an attorney and not told why they were being held.

– According to the National Conference for Community and Justice 2000 Survey of Intergroup Relations in the United States (TAP II), there is cause for optimism when it comes to interracial/interethnic contact. Unfortunately self-reports by respondents indicate discrimination as a common part of many Americans' everyday lives and 79 percent feel that "racial, religious or ethnic tension" is a very serious or somewhat serious problem.

– The Civil Rights Department of Justice has been involved in the investigation of alleged incidents involving violence or threats against Arab Americans, Muslim Americans, Sikh Americans, and South-Asian Americans. The Civil Rights Division, the Federal Bureau of Investigation, and the U.S. Attorneys' offices have investigated approximately 380 such incidents since Sept. 11—three times as many investigations than before Sept. 11.

11 Advocate the immediate control and ultimate elimination of biologic, chemical and nuclear weapons. D

– In November 2001, the United States rejected a protocol aimed at strengthening the 1975 Biological Weapons Convention (BWC). This protocol was developed by an Ad Hoc Group to address concerns about noncompliance. On the last day of the conference, the U.S. attempted to force through a decision to disband the Ad Hoc Group and terminate its mandate. To avoid a collapse of this meeting aimed at bolstering the BWC, parties agreed to suspend work until November 2002. The conference will reconvene Nov. 11, 2002.

– Effective June 13, 2002 the United States terminated its participation in the Anti-Ballistic Missile (ABM) Treaty.

+ As of late 2002, the Chemical Weapons Convention (CWC) has 145 state-party signatories including the United States. The CWC requires not only the elimination of all stocks of chemical weapons but also international monitoring of both government and commercial facilities to verify that Parties were complying with their obligations.

– Although all four declared possessors of chemical weapons are moving forward with their destruction efforts, both Russia and the United States have informed the CWC treaty organization—the Organization for the Prohibition of Chemical Weapons (OPCW)—that they will be unable to meet the April 2007 deadline for destroying their chemical weapons stockpiles. Also, the OPCW is in the second year of a financial crisis, resulting in serious cutbacks in verification activities. During 2001, only 67 percent of the planned inspections were carried out; further cuts in inspections are expected in 2002.

12 Build and sustain the public health capacity to develop systems to collect data about the health and mental health consequences of terrorism and other disasters on victims. B

+ Since fall 2001, CDC has conducted research to learn more about anthrax, how to treat it and how to best mobilize the public health system in the event of an anthrax attack. In addition, follow-up is being conducted to ascertain the current health status of anthrax survivors as well as the nearly 10,000 people who were exposed to anthrax during last fall's attacks and were advised to take a 60-day course of antibiotic prophylaxis.

+ Expanded communications systems—such as the Health Alert Network (HAN) and Epidemic Information Exchange (Epi-X)—are getting vital information to public health workers quickly in late 2002.

+ CDC is evaluating the speed of the health systems response to an outbreak by analyzing the time between the ordering of a blood test by a doctor who suspects a patient is infected with West Nile [virus] and the confirmation of the diagnosis by a state or local health department.

8

Families Can Prepare for Bioterrorism

Bill Frist

Bill Frist is a Republican senator from Tennessee. He is the Senate's only practicing physician and is a former transplant surgeon. He has also written more than one hundred articles and several books. He is a ranking member of the Senate Subcommittee on Public Health and Safety.

The World Trade Center and Pentagon attacks and the anthrax-containing letters of fall 2001 disturbed families throughout the United States, creating feelings of anxiety and helplessness. Families can take important steps to prepare for bioterrorist attacks, however. They can be observant when in public places and provide clear reports of unusual activity to authorities. They can also make plans for communication, evacuation, and preparedness at home that would be useful in the case of any kind of disaster. These plans include preparing a disaster supply kit.

Americans have suddenly had to come face-to-face with the now very real threat of the use of biological and chemical agents against them and their loved ones. The risk is small, tiny in fact. But there is risk, and unfortunately, as recent times have so vividly illustrated, it is increasing.

Everywhere I've gone in 2002, people have asked me what they can do to protect themselves and their loved ones from the threat of bioterrorism. They want to know how to cope effectively with the stress and anxiety it can cause.

Our family has been affected by the events of fall 2001. Every family has. My wife, Karyn, and I have three boys: Bryan, who is fourteen years old; Jonathan, sixteen; and Harrison, eighteen. They watched me live through the frightening uncertainty of the fall 2001 anthrax exposure on Capitol Hill, and I've done my best to address their concerns about the events surrounding September 11, 2001, and the anthrax-laced letter that was mailed to my colleague Senator Tom Daschle.

At their school events, I receive many questions from concerned parents regarding what they should tell their children and how they can help

Bill Frist, *When Every Moment Counts: What You Need to Know About Bioterrorism from the Senate's Only Doctor.* Lanham, MD: Rowman & Littlefield, 2002. Copyright © 2002 by Bill Frist. All rights reserved. Reproduced by permission of the publisher.

them live without fear. My purpose here is to answer as many of those questions as I can, as specifically and practically as I can. . . .

My focus is simply on what families need to know and do to be as prepared as they can be for this threat our nation faces. Just to be clear, there is a huge difference between being prepared and living in fear. One of the most perceptive things I read in the aftermath of the anthrax attacks in fall 2001 was written by columnist Jonathan Alter in *Newsweek*. Recounting his experiences working in the New York offices of NBC when an anthrax-tainted letter was delivered there, Alter wrote, "Anthrax is not contagious, but fear is."

Precisely. There is no reason for paralysis in our everyday lives, and clearly no cause for panic. But there is good reason for every American, young and old, to know much more about what in these times might confront them. *Bio*terrorism personalizes terror like no other type of terrorism. But there are steps each of us can take to reduce our vulnerabilities and thereby restore our sense of security and safety. . . .

Keep your eyes open

When the nation is put on "high alert," what specific actions should I take?

After the September 11 attacks, the federal government issued several notices placing law enforcement agencies and the military on "high alert" when credible information of possible terrorist attacks had been compiled by intelligence sources. At the same time, general alerts were issued to the public.

The alerts are a way for the federal government to let citizens know that the military and law enforcement agencies are increasing their vigilance and that citizens should, too. I know people feel frustrated because they don't know exactly what to do. It can be stressful for them and their families.

Frankly, our government is in a tough spot on this one. If we receive what we believe is credible information regarding a possible terrorist attack—even if key details such as when and where are missing—shouldn't the government let the people know? President George W. Bush believes we should, and I agree.

There is a huge difference between being prepared and living in fear.

But is there really anything you can do to help? Absolutely. First and foremost you can be the eyes and ears of our law enforcement agencies. You know your communities better than anyone else. You know when something looks out of place, whether it's a package left on the subway or someone acting in an unusual or suspicious manner in your neighborhood.

Being more vigilant empowers you to be part of our war to rid the world of the evil of terrorism. Be more conscious of what's going on around you. Report any suspicious activity or behavior to local authorities. But vigilance alone is not enough. You should take additional steps now to plan and prepare for how your family will respond if there is a bioterrorist or some other form of attack.

When I'm in public, what should I look for?

Terrorists tend to choose highly visible targets where large numbers of people gather. These would include large cities, international airports, subway systems, resorts, historic landmarks, and major sporting and entertainment events.

You can be the eyes and ears of our law enforcement agencies.

It's not that people should avoid these places. In fact, it's important that we not give in to fear by allowing the terrorists to change the way we live. Instead, whenever you're in one of these situations, just be a little more aware of your surroundings.

Learn where the emergency exits and staircases are. Plan ahead how you would get out quickly in an emergency.

If you're traveling, take note of any conspicuous or unusual behavior. Don't accept packages from strangers, and never leave your luggage unattended.

What should I do if I find myself in the middle of a scene that might involve biological or chemical materials?

Don't panic! Yes, every situation is different, but there are general steps that will minimize risk to you and your loved ones. And these apply to both biological and chemical events.

1. If you're outside, evaluate the suspected area from a position upwind, cover all exposed skin surfaces, and protect your respiratory system as much as possible, perhaps using a handkerchief to cover your mouth and nose.
2. If the incident is inside, leave immediately and try to avoid the contaminated area on your way out. Keep windows and unused doors closed. Turn off the ventilation system (air-conditioning or heat). If you are inside and the event is outside, stay inside. Turn off the ventilation system and seal windows and doors with plastic tape.
3. Call 911 and report the following:
   - Your name and phone number
   - Date and time of event
   - Distance from the incident or point of impact
   - Reason for the report (for example, people becoming sick, a vapor cloud, dead or sick animals or birds, unusual odors, dead or discolored vegetation)
   - Location of the incident
   - Description of the terrain (for example, flat, hills, river)
   - Weather
   - Temperature
   - Odor (for example, none, sweet, fruity, pepper, garlic, rotten eggs)
   - Visible emission (for example, none, smoke, haze)
   - Symptoms (for example, none, dizziness, runny nose, choking,

tightness in chest, blurred vision, fever, difficulty breathing, stinging of skin, welts/blisters, headaches, nausea, and vomiting) and time they appeared
- Explosion (for example, none, air, ground, structure, underground) and location

4. Once clear of the suspected contaminated area, remove all external clothing and leave it outside. Proceed directly (within minutes) to a shower and thoroughly wash with soap and water, scrubbing aggressively to cover every part of your body with at least ten scrubbing motions. Irrigate your eyes with water.

Plan with your family

What kind of plan do I need for my family?

Every family should have a disaster plan. If yours doesn't, start discussing a plan tonight at the dinner table. Even without the threat of bioterrorism, this is a sound idea. The current world situation only reinforces the need for preparedness. We're not talking about bomb shelters here or the pre-Y2K hysteria to which some fell prey. The things you should do to safeguard your family in case of a bioterrorist attack are basically the same as what you would do for any natural disaster.

Your plan should cover three essential elements, according to the American Red Cross:
- Communication: How will you communicate with family members if there is a bioterrorist attack or some other disaster?
- Destination: Where will your family go if there is an attack?
- Supplies: What supplies should you have on hand in case you need to "shelter at home" for a while?

What kind of communications plan do I need?

Choose one person who lives out of state to be your family's contact in case of emergency. Why? In a disaster, it's often easier to call long distance than to make a local call. Everyone in your family should know the phone number.

Also, choose a family meeting place outside your neighborhood in case you can't go home. Again, everyone in your family should know the address and phone number.

In addition, you should have a backup out-of-state contact and a backup meeting place, just for insurance. And be sure to discuss your plan routinely with family members so that it becomes second nature. That will help prevent panic if disaster does strike.

Every family should have a disaster plan.

Where should my family go if there's a bioterrorist attack?

That obviously will depend on how close the attack occurs to your home. The most likely scenario appears to be that emergency officials would urge people to shelter at home in the event of a bioterrorist attack. So designate a "safe room" in your home, one with a telephone and radio. Choose an interior room without windows, if possible. Don't use the basement, however, because—in a chemical attack—heavier chemical vapors would tend to sink to the lowest place in a house. Gather your family in the safe room and listen to the news for further instructions.

If officials order an evacuation, make sure everyone in your family knows in advance how to get outside from every room in the house. Where possible, devise two escape routes from every room, in case one is blocked.

Prepare a disaster kit

What about disaster supply kits? What supplies should I have in case of a bioterror attack?

Disaster supply kits are just what they imply: a collection of basic supplies that are readily available in the event there is a "worst-case scenario" that requires you and your family to become fully self-sufficient for several days. In the case of bioterrorism, this might occur because stores are closed and other social services interrupted. The disaster kit for bioterrorism is not very different from that required for other types of emergencies.

The disaster kit for bioterrorism is not very different from that required for other types of emergencies.

Pack essential supplies in an easy-to-carry container such as a large, covered trash can, a duffel bag, or a camping backpack. Store this disaster supply kit where it can be easily reached, and make sure every family member knows where it is. That way, you can grab it quickly whether you have to remain inside or evacuate.

Your disaster supply kit should include the following items:
- Water. Store in plastic containers such as large soft-drink bottles. Have at least a three-day supply, figuring on one gallon a day for each person. Change the water in your kit at least every six months.
- Canned food. At least a three-day supply. Good items include canned meats, fruits, and vegetables; juices, milk, and soups; high-energy snacks such as peanut butter, jelly, crackers, "power bars," and trail mix; candy and cookies; instant coffee and tea bags; and any special foods for infants, the elderly, or those on special diets. Avoid salty items, though, as they will make you drink more water. Write the date on the food items and change foods at least every six months. Be sure to check expiration dates on labels. An easy way to remember to update your water and food supplies is to change items at the beginning and end of daylight savings time, when you also change the batteries in smoke detectors.
- Nonelectric can opener.
- Cell phone.
- Change of clothing. One extra set of clothes and footwear for each member of the family.
- Goggles. One pair for each member of the family, to protect the eyes. Swimmer's goggles are fine.
- Respirators for each family member. These are filtered fiber masks

and only cost about $1 each. Look for ones with N95 certification.
- Roll of plastic tape, such as package-sealing tape (to seal windows, if necessary).
- Flashlight with extra batteries.
- Portable radio with extra batteries.
- Portable heater.
- Thermal blankets or sleeping bags. One for each member of the family.
- Extra car keys, credit card, and cash.
- Extra pair of eyeglasses.
- Special items for infants or elderly or disabled family members.
- First aid kit, including:
  - A ten-day supply of your family's prescription medications
  - Painkillers, such as ibuprofen, acetaminophen, or aspirin
  - Antihistamines, if family members have allergies
  - Mild laxative
  - Antidiarrhea medication, such as Pepto-Bismol, Kaopectate, or Imodium AD

If you have pets, include the following items in your supply kit:
- Identification collar and rabies tag
- Carrier or cage
- Leash
- Medications
- Newspapers, litter, trash bags for waste
- Two-week supply of food and water
- Veterinary records (necessary if your pet has to go to a shelter)

9

The Public Is Likely to Respond Well in a Bioterror Attack

Thomas A. Glass and Monica Schoch-Spana

Thomas A. Glass and Monica Schoch-Spana both belong to Johns Hopkins University's Bloomberg School of Public Health in Baltimore, Maryland. Glass works for the school's Center on Aging and Health and Department of Epidemiology, and Schoch-Spana works for the Center for Civilian Biodefense Studies.

Bioterrorism policy discussions have tended to assume that nonprofessional citizens will be a passive factor or an actual impediment in the response to an attack, but this probably will not be the case. Planners should see mass panic as both rare and preventable and should make the public an active partner in proposed response schemes. Individuals and groups providing at-home care are likely to provide important augmentation of hospital care. The chances that the public will respond well can be increased by providing people with accurate information and building public trust. In turn, health officials and policymakers need to trust, value, and make use of public support rather than relying exclusively on professional "first responders."

B ioterrorism policy discussions and response planning efforts have tended to discount the capacity of the public to participate in the response to an act of bioterrorism, or they have assumed that local populations would impede an effective response. Fears of mass panic and social disorder underlie this bias. Although it is not known how the population will react to an unprecedented act of bioterrorism, experience with natural and technological disasters and disease outbreaks indicates a pattern of generally effective and adaptive collective action. Failure to involve the public as a key partner in the medical and public-health response could hamper effective management of an epidemic and increase the likelihood of social disruption. Ultimately, actions taken by nonprofessional indi-

Thomas A. Glass and Monica Schoch-Spana, "Bioterrorism and the People: How to Vaccinate a City Against Panic," *Clinical Infectious Diseases*, vol. 24, January 15, 2002, pp. 217–23. Copyright © 2002 by The University of Chicago. Reproduced by permission.

viduals and groups could have the greatest influence on the outcome of a bioterrorism event. Five guidelines for integrating the public into bioterrorism response planning are proposed: (1) treat the public as a capable ally in the response to an epidemic, (2) enlist civic organizations in practical public health activities, (3) anticipate the need for home-based patient care and infection control, (4) invest in public outreach and communication strategies, and (5) ensure that planning reflects the values and priorities of affected populations.

With more sophisticated awareness of the challenges posed by an epidemic caused by an act of biological terrorism (bioterrorism), the definition of a "first responder" to such an event is necessarily evolving. Infectious disease and infection control specialists, emergency department physicians and nurses, public health officials, epidemiologists, laboratorians, and hospital administrators are now seen as the frontline professionals. The current, professionalized model of the response to bioterrorism, however, has largely cast the civilian population as nonparticipants. Rare are the calls to prepare the public to respond in their own right. Likely contributing to the neglect of the public's role in a response to bioterrorism is the assumption that the general public tends to be irrational, uncoordinated, and uncooperative in emergencies—not to mention prone to panic. Such a view, we argue, will lead public health professionals and emergency managers to miss the opportunity to harness the capacities of the civilian population to enhance the effectiveness of a large-scale response.

As demonstrated by community reactions to the terrorist attacks in New York and Washington, D.C., in late 2001, the power of the public to respond effectively to disasters should not be underestimated. In New York, individual volunteers and organized groups converged on the epicenter of destruction to offer aid and support, despite hazardous conditions and uncertainty about the risks of further attack or structural collapse of the World Trade Center towers. Volunteers responded rapidly and in large numbers to help in search and rescue efforts while professional operations were yet to be put in place. Since the attacks, affected communities have been organizing through local government, relief groups, and civic organizations, such as churches, neighborhood associations, and labor organizations.

Failure to involve the public as a key partner in the medical and public-health response could hamper effective management of an epidemic.

A catastrophic epidemic caused by a bioterrorist attack could produce similar crisis conditions, although of a wholly different nature that will require the participation of nonprofessionals in the emergency response. Preparedness programs would benefit now from discussions about how to capitalize on the effectiveness and resourcefulness of nonprofessionals, especially in the identification, surveillance, and containment of an outbreak, and, potentially, in caring for large numbers of casualties. To that end, we offer 5 guidelines for enhancing the planning for responses to bioterrorism by improving the integration of the lay public. In the [viewpoint's] final section, we offer a preliminary assessment of the general public's responses to the currently unfolding anthrax threat, as the responses bear upon the proposed guiding principles.

See panic as rare and preventable

Discussion of how the general public might respond after a bioterrorist attack typically focuses on the possibility of mass panic, psychological trauma, and social disorder. Creating panic is among the probable goals of those who plan acts of bioterrorism. Expert guides on the health consequences of a bioterrorist attack predominantly focus on negative psychological reactions and aberrant social behaviors. Constructive or salutary responses are rarely highlighted. Scenarios for response exercises routinely feature rioting, looting, and vigilantism. There is a widespread belief that panic and civil unrest are likely in the aftermath of a bioterrorist attack, although it is not known how the general population will react to a unprecedented biological attack. However, research on population responses to a wide range of natural and technological disasters suggests that there is a tendency toward adaptability and cooperation and that lawless behavior is infrequent. Precipitate, unreasoning fear has been found in such rare circumstances as entrapment in a burning structure from which there is no visible means of escape. A study of the 1918 Spanish influenza pandemic suggests that, in a catastrophic epidemic, the general response of the public is also one of resourcefulness, civility, and mutual aid.

> *There is a tendency toward adaptability and cooperation and . . . lawless behavior is infrequent.*

The view that panic is the "natural" response of groups in extreme peril ignores the fact that behavioral responses are context sensitive. Collective behavior changes over time and in relation to external events. This suggests that, in times of disaster, panic may be "iatrogenic": that is, the actions of emergency managers may determine the extent and duration of panic, to the extent it exists. For example, public reactions to an outbreak of meningitis [an infectious brain disease] suggest that infectious disease and infection control specialists who routinely deal with contagion can help prevent panic by using the mass media and personal outreach in neighborhoods and at people's workplaces to provide credible, practical information on how to minimize the risk of disease transmission. Public information strategies aimed at demystifying the world of microbes, as well as instruction in personal protective practices, reinforce the public's sense of control, and would be important steps toward "vaccinating" the public against panic. This argument is bolstered by research on factors known to provoke and amplify worry, fear, helplessness, and anger in threatening situations.

The image of a panicked mob makes exciting footage in disaster movies, but it obscures a broad range of possible public reactions. The empirical study of collective behavior during disasters documents stress, fear, depression, and other negative responses, but it also points to emergent patterns of action that show cooperation, adaptiveness, and resourcefulness. Often, behavior that is not sanctioned by officials is erroneously defined as panic, rather than as an effective response of resourceful people acting in concert. Officials may be inclined to see a "command-and-control" model of disaster management as the only rational approach. In 1979, when a partial meltdown occurred at the nuclear power plant at Three Mile Island (south of Harrisbug, PA), almost 40% of the population within 15 miles of the nuclear plant evacuated the area on their own. In the absence of clear information or leadership from public safety officials, residents made the reasonable decision to remove themselves from a situation of unknown and potentially significant risk, and they did so effectively and without evidence of panic.

Nonprofessionals in the immediate vicinity have saved the majority of people rescued from disasters.

Further protection against social disorganization and panic is provided by deeply ingrained norms of civility and sociality. For instance, panic was rare in the stairwells of the World Trade Center when it was bombed in 1993. The calm and orderly evacuation of the towers was aided by the fact that people in the buildings knew each other from working together and sharing the same office floor. Because of these social ties and the perception that exits and stairways were accessible, groups of office workers cooperated in vacating the building calmly and efficiently. Initial reports about the evacuation of the World Trade Center during the attack that occurred on 11 September 2001 suggest that people's responses were equally clearheaded and cooperative. This study and others have shown that standards of civil behavior prevail even in the most challenging circumstances. Social chaos does not occur in disaster situations because people tend to respond in accordance with their customary norms and roles (e.g., the able-bodied assist the impaired, supervisors assume responsibility for the safety of those they supervise, and friends look out for friends). This finding suggests that plans for a response to bioterrorism should attempt, whenever possible, to recognize and capitalize on existing social relations. For example, if quarantine should be necessary, establishing cohorts of individuals who are already known to one other in some capacity might be better than creating clusters of strangers.

History demonstrates that large-scale, fatal epidemics of previously unknown disease can create significant social disruption early in the outbreak. Such disruption can include unwarranted fear of exposure to the disease, suspicion of others, and stigmatization of individuals or groups who have become infected or are presumed to be carriers of disease. However, these effects tend to become less severe as communities develop routines and strategies for coping, even during epidemics of such horrific diseases as the plague in 14th-century Europe and HIV/AIDS today. This finding suggests that effective communication strategies will be needed early during the outbreak and that substantial planning may be necessary far in advance of an incident.

Make the public a partner

Emergency services personnel, when focused on executing their professional duties, tend to think of the public as passive bystanders who are dispensible to the business of response. To the extent that medical resources exceed the medical needs of a specific event, this view is reasonable. At the scene of a traffic accident, for example, members of the general public are separated from the response operation by the familiar barrier of yellow tape. By definition, however, a disaster is an event that generates casualties in excess of available resources. In those specific circumstances, this "yellow-tape phenomenon" is vestigial. Data show that ordinary, nonprofessional citizens are capable of full and useful participation in times of crisis. In general, nonprofessionals in the immediate vicinity have saved the majority of people rescued in disasters, greatly aiding the work of the professionals who respond.

It makes little sense to talk about the "general public" as if it is a single entity, in the same way that it makes little sense to talk about a single U.S. health care "system." The general public is comprised of an interconnected matrix of networks and subnetworks organized around social institutions and relationships. Individuals are members of organizations and groups whose social ties, resources, communication links, and leadership structures might be used to facilitate a better and more coordinated response after a terrorist attack. Examples of these networks include civic networks (e.g., churches, social clubs, and schools), occupational networks (e.g., businesses, labor unions, and professional organizations), and information networks (e.g., libraries and Internet chat rooms and bulletin boards). Each network can be thought of as a potential conduit for organizing or facilitating public responses that are beneficial. For example, church groups might distribute antibiotics, convene vaccination meetings, or arrange visits to the homes of people who are ill. Social groups, such as the Kiwanis or Rotary Clubs, might activate phone trees to gather case reports, trace contacts, or disseminate instructions on appropriate use of medications.

What is needed is a plan that includes the possibility of home-based treatment and supportive care arrangements to augment hospital-based care.

Planning for bioterrorism response has not, to date, defined a role for the public in disease surveillance, even though the general public historically has been an accurate source of reports of infectious disease outbreaks. Rumor-reporting systems and emergency telephone hotlines—2 channels of information from the general population—have been invaluable to epidemiological investigations and efforts to trace contacts, and they have been important sources of information on the adverse effects of vaccines and antibiotics administered to control outbreaks. As suggested by the Spanish influenza pandemic of 1918, the role of the general public in providing outbreak data becomes all the more critical in the context of a catastrophic epidemic. Health care providers and institutions may be so consumed with caring for casualties that they will not be able to devote sufficient time or resources to the tracking of new cases of disease.

Not only is it possible to imagine networks of public responders that can aid in information dissemination, outbreak monitoring, resource distribution, and even patient care, but, in the midst of a collective crisis, a positive and active role for community groups and individual citizens provides a potential antidote to panic and other adverse psychological effects. In times of crisis, having a constructive role to play engages people in a common mission and provides a sense of control in periods of grave uncertainty.

Plan for at-home care

Much planning for bioterrorism response has been guilty of double myopia [nearsightedness]. First, it has assumed that the formal hospital system will be capable of managing the disaster alone. Second, it has assumed that the general public is incapable of playing a role in the medical response. During the past decade, mergers, downsizing, workforce shortages, and the shift toward outpatient services have reduced the number of hospital beds drastically in all major medical marketplaces. The existing network of hospitals probably would not be capable of adequately caring for the people affected by a large-scale bioterrorist attack. Because hospitals function according to a "just-in-time" management principle for nursing, medicine, and equipment, they typically do not have the capacity to handle patient loads that are greater than projected. Hospitals, in general, lack the capacity to cope with an unexpected surge of patients. In the aftermath of a significant bioterrorism event, overburdened hospitals may be forced to turn patients away, discharge those who are the least ill, and ration finite supplies and personnel; each of these responses occurred during the 1918 influenza pandemic.

Plans have been made at the national level, as part of the Domestic Preparedness Program, for the mobilization of military teams and mobile medical care facilities; however, in most major U.S. cities, in even a small outbreak of epidemic disease, hospital-bed capacity could be exceeded quickly. Whatever partnerships might be imagined between clinics, hospitals, the Veterans Administration hospital system, and other inpatient care systems, hospitals could plausibly reach the limits of their functional capacity. What is needed is a plan that includes the possibility of home-based treatment and supportive care arrangements to augment hospital-based care. The majority of victims of the Spanish influenza outbreak of 1918, for example, were cared for at home by family, neighbors, Red Cross volunteers, visiting nurses, and hospital social workers, among others.

Information on responses to infectious disease emergencies is not, however, the only source of evidence in favor of a decentralized response. Professional health services are only a small percentage of the total care that patients receive on a regular basis. Family members and other lay nonprofessionals provide the vast majority (70%–90%) of routine care in communities. Emergency plans for distributing to the general public resources and information about nutrition, sanitation, infection control, and the care of seriously ill persons could be of great value in a response to bioterrorism. For instance, a network of community information centers was critical to the functioning of Israel's emergency health system during the Persian Gulf War in 1991; these centers dispensed medical information, medication instructions, and reports indicating which hospitals, clinics, and pharmacies were open.

Provide accurate information

Review of relevant historical examples suggests that effective leadership and delivery of clear, credible, and timely information both during and after a bioterrorist attack would be critical components of a response. In the face of uncertainty, the general public would need reassurance, descriptions of the response measures under way, instruction in personal and collective protective measures, and messages of hope. Infectious disease professionals (along with emergency managers) would have a critical role in helping to distribute this information in a timely and credible manner, which might significantly lessen the impact of a bioterrorist attack. On the other hand, the release of inaccurate, confusing, or contradictory information by leaders and/or the media has the potential to increase levels of fear, panic, and demoralization, as well as to discredit authorities. Moreover, failures of communication among government officials, health experts, and citizens can create misunderstanding, suspicion, and resistance that ultimately inhibit efforts to halt the spread of disease.

Considerable resources are required to disseminate information to the public in an emergency, as was demonstrated during a recent outbreak of West Nile virus in New York City in 1999. Health officials and emergency managers conducted a massive campaign to educate the public through daily press conferences, regular media releases, a telephone hotline, Web-site updates, multilingual brochures and fliers, and personal contact at the epicenter of the outbreak. This campaign severely strained existing human resources, underscoring the problem of surge capacity for health departments. Telephone hotline staff, 25–75 of whom were required per shift, answered telephone calls for 24 hours each day and fielded a total of more than 150,000 inquiries during a period of 7 weeks. A significant bioterrorist attack certainly would generate more calls than were made in the New York City area during the West Nile virus outbreak. Gathering data on the most frequently asked questions could be one step toward building a more responsive public information strategy.

Along with the need for a pharmaceutical stockpile of vaccines and antibiotics, there is an urgent need for an information stockpile.

A bioterrorist attack is likely to produce a climate of grave uncertainty and insecurity. As has been the case in historic epidemics, the general public will try to make sense of the experience of sudden, widespread disease. Questions such as "Why?" "Why me?" "What next?" and "How and when will this end?" will abound. Public health officials should anticipate the need to provide accurate and timely information about the nature of the attack and the steps that are being taken to mitigate its effects. Reporting systems that track the scope of the epidemic will be critical to these efforts. At the same time, health authorities should also be open and candid about the limits of available information and resources. To the extent that the general public perceives that public health officials are failing to provide accurate appraisals of the outbreak's scope and impact, a credibility gap will open rapidly, causing individuals to seek alternative (and perhaps less accurate) sources of information. Evidence from the public health response to the anthrax outbreaks in late 2001 illustrates the deleterious impact on public trust that can result from what John Schwartz of the *New York Times* has referred to as the "spin-control" model of public information release—that is, a risk-averse approach that avoids full and complete disclosure in order to minimize potential negative political consequences of actual or perceived errors with respect to a response.

The public will not take the pill if it does not trust the doctor.

Public health officials should also expect requests to list specific steps that individuals can take to lower their risk of either being exposed to infectious agents or transmitting them. Along with the need for a pharmaceutical stockpile of vaccines and antibiotics, there is an urgent need for an information stockpile, including public service announcements about infectious disease concepts (e.g., contagion and the value of vaccination), infection control procedures to be followed at home, and information for the public in the event of the need for quarantine. Official spokespersons need to be prepared to discuss both the benefits and the risks of epidemic control measures while clearly advocating the need for recommended actions. Health officials and hospital administrators need to be prepared to indicate which hospitals and clinics are capable of taking patients and where other critical medical resources exist. Efforts to provide adequate information will undoubtedly be complicated by the shifting sands of what is known and the interruptions in the flow of information that characterize all public emergencies.

Build public trust

The public will not take the pill if it does not trust the doctor. Stopping a disease outbreak will require that public health professionals and government leaders carefully nurture the general population's trust and confidence in the institutions of public health and government and their actions, especially if large-scale disease containment measures are necessary. After a bioterrorist attack, public trust could be a fragile asset, yet it is essential. The issue of trust bears significantly on 2 critical aspects of the medical and public health response to bioterrorism: (1) the choice of strategies for effective communication with the public, and (2) the processes for debating, as a society, some of the more ethically complex dimensions of disease containment.

Although there is a tendency to view the media as an impediment to emergency response, a bioterrorist attack would necessitate a close working relationship between the media, decision-makers, and those involved in response operations. Given the speed with which news reports circulate today, and given the importance of the media in shaping public responses, health departments and hospitals would need to be responsive to media requests for information. An important step toward maintaining an effective, nonadversarial relationship with the press is to have more routine interactions with reporters, producers, and editorial boards before periods of crisis. During an emergency, health professionals could then build on their relationship with the media to effectively disseminate an accurate account of events, provide vital disease control information, and communicate the rationale and justification for the necessary medical and public health responses.

Mass media outlets can get vital information to the largest numbers of people the most quickly. However, the mass media and the Internet are not sufficient. Additional communication strategies would be critical to enlisting the public as partners in implementing epidemic controls. Multilingual materials and culturally relevant messages that are endorsed and delivered by persons who have local respect and authority can help ensure that control measures are successfully disseminated to all sectors of a diverse community. Direct personal contact has the most significant effect on a person's willingness to trust and act on health-related information. Public outreach strategies of health departments and emergency services should include interpersonal exchanges of information—for example, town meetings and public workshops. On the other hand, the realities of an outbreak of a disease that is propagated by person-to-person transmission would require alternatives to such public meetings. Under those circumstances, means of remote communication (e.g., "telephone trees," Internet-based communications, and newsletters) would be important alternatives.

The extent to which the general public supports large-scale, potentially disruptive disease containment measures may also depend on the transparency and accessibility of the decision-making process. Accounts of historic epidemics demonstrate that extreme containment measures, such as quarantine, can be perceived as being more problematic than the disease itself. During an outbreak of polio in 1916 in a Long Island community, a large citizens' group protested the sometimes forcible removal of sick children from the care of parents to an isolation hospital. Enlisting the public as partners in disaster response would likely require the use of participatory decision-making bodies, such as citizen advisory panels, for responses that require a community's ethical judgment (e.g., setting priorities for use of scarce medical resources, such as antibiotics and vaccines). Strategies for public discourse and a participatory and transparent decision-making process in the midst of an epidemic might involve enlisting leaders of local religious organizations or labor groups to provide feedback about proposed epidemic control measures.

Trust the public's response

Resourceful, adaptive behavior is the rule rather than the exception in communities beset by technological and natural disasters as well as epidemics. As planning for responses to acts of bioterrorism evolves, it is important to develop strategies that enlist the public as essential and capable partners. The 2001 terrorist attacks in New York and Washington, D.C., draw attention to the important role of nonprofessional individuals and groups in the immediate and long-term response to disasters with mass casualties that cannot be contained within a perimeter of yellow tape. Involving the public will require, in part, raising of the general public's awareness of their roles and responsibilities after a biological attack.

Resourceful, adaptive behavior is the rule rather than the exception in communities beset by technological and natural disasters as well as epidemics.

The complexity of people's reactions to the anthrax-tainted letters discovered after the 11 September tragedies further undermines any simple notions we might have about the general population's ability to cope with a bioterrorism crisis. What began as a single case of inhalational anthrax had become, by late November 2001, an outbreak with 23 total cases of infection and 5 deaths that had disrupted the U.S. Congress, the Supreme Court, and the U.S. Postal Service. The exhortations of news editors, politicians, and pundits, which urged the public not to panic and to go about their daily routines, suggest how fearful decision-makers were about the potential for public hysteria. A preliminary assessment of events, however, indicates a temperate, if complex, response by the general public.

In the aftermath of the September 11 attacks, increases in the purchase of gas masks and ciprofloxacin were quickly seen. What was described as "panic buying" in some reports may have been a reasonable attempt to acquire protection in the face of stark, proven vulnerability to terrorism. Moreover, what appears to some as panic may be evidence of the public's resourcefulness when advice from professionals is confusing or nonexistent. Concerns about providing children with gas masks that fit and with correct doses of antibiotics also suggest that the public is not prone to panic but has a deep-seated need to seek protection for the most vulnerable members of society.

Health officials' warnings about the potential dangers of off-the-shelf respirators and personal drug stockpiles have also met a generally receptive audience. Seven of 10 individuals who were surveyed in a Gallup poll conducted on 21 October 2001 indicated that they had not thought about buying a gas mask or obtaining a prescription for antibiotics. This and a second poll characterize the response of the general public as one of "reasoned calm" and "reluctance to panic." As 2001 nears its end, closer proximity to danger has not yet given rise to unreasoning fear and erratic behavior. In late October, a poll of Florida residents found that more than 50% had little or no concern about contracting anthrax. Reports of mass testing and prophylaxis at affected work sites indicate that the process was orderly, as hundreds and sometimes thousands of individuals waited in line for their turn.

Increased vigilance regarding personal safety has resulted in a significant burden on professional responders. During October 2001, the Federal Bureau of Investigation investigated more than 2500 suspected anthrax attacks, many of which were reports by concerned citizens about harmless substances. The health care system has also fielded an increasing number of demands for diagnostic tests by individuals who fear they may have been exposed to anthrax. However, when seen in the context of conflicting reports from experts about the nature of the threat, as well as vague and nonspecific government alerts about additional possible attacks, the level of public concern appears measured and reasonable.

In short, evidence that the public cannot be trusted with full, accurate disclosure of what is known about a bioterrorist threat is lacking. The events of 11 September 2001 and after further undermine the view that the public is prone to panic, incapable of effective participation, and inclined to respond irrationally. How the public responds to this and any future threat of bioterrorism may depend, to a considerable degree, on how and to what extent decision-makers activate strategies that "vaccinate" against the risk that the public will distrust them, will rely on misinformation, and will be excluded from participation in decision-making.

10

Everyone Should Be Vaccinated Against Smallpox

Charles Krauthammer

Charles Krauthammer is a regular columnist for the Washington Post. *He won the Pulitzer Prize for distinguished commentary in 1987.*

The government's plan to make smallpox vaccinations voluntary for health care workers and discourage vaccination for the general public does not go far enough. People who choose not to be vaccinated and catch smallpox during a bioterror attack endanger not only themselves but others because they can spread the disease. Vaccination for everyone should be made mandatory, just as vaccination for childhood diseases is now mandatory, in order to protect society.

The eradication of smallpox was one of humanity's great success stories. After thousands of years of suffering at the hands of the virus, the human race gathered all its wit and cunning and conquered the scourge, eradicating it forever [in the late 1970s]. Well, forever lasted less than 25 years. It does not bode well for the future of our species that it took but a blink of the eye for one of history's worst killers to make a comeback—not on its own, mind you, but brought back by humans to kill again.

During the age of innocence—the '90s, during which it seemed history had ended—the big debate was whether the two remaining known stocks of smallpox in the world, one in Russia and the other in the U.S., should be destroyed. It seemed like a wonderful idea, except that no one could be absolutely sure that some smallpox stores had not fallen into other hands. In fact, [in 2002] we now think Iraq is working on weaponizing smallpox, and perhaps North Korea and others too.

The danger is greater now than ever—first, and ironically, because of our very success in eradicating it in the past. People today have almost no experience with, and therefore no immunity to, the virus. We are nearly as virgin a population as the Native Americans who were wiped out by

Charles Krauthammer, "Smallpox Shots: Make Them Mandatory," *Time*, vol. 160, December 23, 2002, p. 84. Copyright © 2002 by Time, Inc. Reproduced by permission.

the various deadly pathogens brought over by Europeans. Not content with that potential for mass murder, however, today's bad guys are reportedly trying to genetically manipulate the virus to make it even deadlier and more resistant to treatment. Who knows what monstrosities the monsters are brewing in their secret laboratories.

Vaccination is the conscription of civilians in the war against bioterrorism.

What to do? We have enough vaccine on hand, some diluted but still effective, to vaccinate everyone in the U.S., with more full-strength versions to come. President [George W.] Bush has just announced [in late 2002] that his Administration will take the concentric-circle approach: mandatory inoculations for certain soldiers, voluntary inoculations for medical and emergency workers, and then inoculations available to, but discouraged for, everybody else.

It sounds good, but it is not quite right. If smallpox were a threat just to individuals, then it could be left up to individuals to decide whether or not they want to protect themselves. When it comes to epidemic diseases, however, we don't leave it up to individuals to decide. The state decides.

Forget about smallpox. This happens every day with childhood diseases. No child can go to school unless he's been immunized. Parents have no choice. Think of it: we force parents to inject healthy children with organisms—some living, some dead—that in a small number of cases will cripple or kill the child. It is an extraordinary violation of the privacy and bodily integrity of the little citizen. Yet it is routine. Why? Because what is at stake is the vulnerability of the entire society to catastrophic epidemic. In that case, individuals must submit.

Which is why smallpox vaccines were mandatory when we were kids. It wasn't left up to you to decide if you wanted it. You might be ready to risk your life by forgoing the vaccine, but society would not let you—not because it was saving you from yourself but because it had to save others from you. The problem wasn't you getting smallpox; the problem was you giving smallpox to others if you got it. Society cannot tolerate that. We forced vaccination even though we knew it would maim and kill a small but certain number of those subjected to it.

Today [in 2002] the case for mandatory vaccination is even stronger. This is war. We need to respond as in war. The threat is not just against individuals, but against the nation. Smallpox kills a third of its victims. If this epidemic were to take hold, it could devastate America as a functioning society. And the government's highest calling is to protect society—a calling even higher than protecting individuals.

That is why conscription in wartime is justified. We violate the freedom of individuals by drafting them into combat, risking their lives—suspending, in effect, their right to life and liberty, to say nothing of the pursuit of happiness—in the name of the nation.

Vaccination is the conscription of civilians in the war against bioterrorism. I personally would choose not to receive the smallpox vaccine. I would not have my family injected. I prefer the odds of getting the disease vs. the odds of inflicting injury or death by vaccination on my perfectly healthy child.

Nonetheless, it should not be my decision. When what is at stake is the survival of the country, personal and family calculation must yield to national interest. And a population fully protected from smallpox is a supreme national interest.

If it is determined that the enemy really has smallpox and might use it, we should vaccinate everyone. We haven't been called upon to do very much for the country since [the terrorist attacks on] Sept. 11, 2001. We can and should do this.

11

Individuals Should Decide Whether to Be Vaccinated Against Smallpox

Charles V. Peña

Charles V. Peña is senior defense policy analyst and director of defense policy studies at the Cato Institute, a nonprofit public policy research foundation in Washington, D.C. His opinions have appeared in numerous newspapers, magazines, and e-zines.

Vaccinating people against smallpox after cases have already appeared might have worked for natural outbreaks, but it is unlikely to be a good strategy if smallpox is used as a bioterrorist weapon because there will not be time or facilities for mass vaccination. Instead, the smallpox vaccine should be made available to the public as soon as possible, and individuals should decide whether to be vaccinated based on their health status and perception of risks versus benefits. Even if only a portion of the population is vaccinated, this will create a "community immunity" that will slow the rate of disease transmission and buy time to vaccinate others after an attack has occurred.

The Centers for Disease Control (CDC) will hold closed meetings in mid-2002 on what to do about possible bioterrorism and the smallpox vaccine. Americans are smart enough to choose whether to take the vaccine and therefore it should be made available to the public.

Unfortunately, the current policy leaves Americans with no choice in the matter—no freedom to choose what may be most effective for their own security and peace of mind. In the case of a bioterrorist attack using smallpox, Americans cannot immunize themselves beforehand with the vaccine. The government won't give its own citizens access to the vaccine, even though it's in stock and even though Vice President Cheney's comments on terrorism in early 2002 show that the threat of smallpox bioterrorism is real.

That's unacceptable.

Charles V. Peña, "Give Americans the Choice to Take the Smallpox Vaccine," www.foxnews.com, June 5, 2002. Copyright © 2002 by FOX News Online. Reproduced by permission.

At its June 19–20, 2002, meeting, the CDC will likely produce policy guidance for smallpox vaccination. [Editor's note: The CDC subsequently recommended vaccinating first responders but not the general public.] The CDC should decide against perpetuating the "ring containment" strategy accepted until this time, whereby government doles out smallpox vaccinations only after a known outbreak in the hope of containing the spread of the virus. That may make sense for a natural outbreak in a rural area, but such a policy would likely be disastrous against smallpox bioterrorism.

Don't gamble with smallpox

Although eradicated as a disease in 1978—the government had mandated vaccination of all children with the vaccine—smallpox is a devastating virus. It has a 30 percent or higher fatality rate among unvaccinated persons (Americans born after 1972 have not been vaccinated) and is easily transmitted. Smallpox has killed more people than any other infectious disease in human history and in the 20th century killed three times more people than all the wars combined (400 million vs. 111 million).

Compared to the anthrax-laden letters distributed in the mail in fall 2001, the smallpox virus is easier to disperse. It can be aerosolized and released into the air in a crowded place such as a shopping mall, sports stadium, or airport. The virus need not even be weaponized. Suicide terrorists could infect themselves with the virus and transmit it to others by coughing and sneezing, which can release millions of deadly virus particles though the air.

The government won't give its own citizens access to the vaccine.

Indeed, a smallpox attack could occur at multiple locations and may not be immediately known (the initial symptoms are flu-like and it could be 12 or more days before smallpox is diagnosed). As a result, the virus could spread widely and kill thousands before the first vaccinations are administered (the vaccine must be given within 4 days of being exposed to be effective). Moreover, given a dense and highly mobile population, the virus is likely to spread much faster and wider (including to other countries) than a ring containment strategy can keep up with. And in the inevitable post-attack panic and confusion, the medical infrastructure would be overwhelmed by millions of people demanding immediate vaccination.

Rather than leaving the entire population at risk and responding to a smallpox attack after the fact, a better approach would be to take preventative measures before an attack occurs. In mid-2002 the U.S. government is in possession of 15 million doses of smallpox vaccine that, according to a study published by the *New England Journal of Medicine*, can be effectively diluted 5-fold (perhaps as much as 10 times). Combined with some 85 million additional doses of newly discovered smallpox vaccine, there is a sufficient supply of vaccine to allow for voluntary vaccination (with vaccine previously ordered, the smallpox vaccine supply should be about 450 million doses by the end of 2002).

Because there are known risks with the smallpox vaccination (in particular for pregnant women and those with weakened immune systems), individuals should be allowed to make a voluntary, informed decision (in consultation with a doctor) to understand, manage, and mitigate those risks. But the government's withholding of the vaccine until after an attack—forcing people to make the stark choice of having to accept the risks of vaccination or be exposed to the deadly smallpox virus—is not an acceptable policy in a society that values individual life and liberty.

Even if only a fraction of the population were vaccinated beforehand, a "community immunity" effect would occur that lowers the rate of transmission of the disease and significantly increases the chances of success of a ring containment strategy. As a result, the chances of a successful attack would be lowered, which could also have a deterrent effect and thus might prevent such an attack from occurring. But that won't happen if Americans aren't given the freedom to choose the vaccine.

Vice President Cheney warned, "The prospects of a future attack against the United States are almost certain." Even a partially vaccinated population against smallpox is more effective than leaving Americans unprotected and at risk, hoping that a pound of cure will work after the fact.

12

Only "First Responders" Should Be Vaccinated Against Smallpox

White House

The White House issues information from the executive branch of the U.S. government.

The federal government's smallpox vaccination program is proposing to vaccinate only health care workers and other "first responders," such as police and firefighters, who might make up response teams who would treat others in the event of a bioterrorist attack using smallpox. The government will monitor and attempt to minimize side effects, but because severe reactions are likely to occur in a small number of people, preattack vaccination for the public as a whole is not recommended. Nonetheless, vaccine will be made available to those who insist on being vaccinated.

Why vaccinate health care workers and first responders?
We're asking these groups to volunteer to serve on smallpox response teams to help our country respond in the event of an attack. By vaccinating groups of health care workers and emergency responders, we will make sure that smallpox response teams are available who can vaccinate others and provide critical services in the days following an attack. This approach will make us better able to protect the American people in an emergency, which is our highest priority.

What will the smallpox response teams do?
Members of the Smallpox Response Teams will include people who will administer the smallpox vaccine in the event of an emergency and will be the first to investigate and evaluate initial suspected case(s) of smallpox and initiate measures to control the outbreak.

The Department of Health and Human Services (HHS) and the Centers for Disease Control and Prevention (CDC) will continue to advise and assist states in development of these teams.

White House, "Frequently Asked Questions," www.whitehouse.gov, December 2002.

How will the government decide who should serve on a smallpox response team?

State officials—in consultation with CDC and local health departments—are working to identify health care workers and first responders who could serve on response teams following a smallpox release. Participation on these teams and in the vaccination program is purely voluntary.

How many first responders and health care workers will be vaccinated?

We have asked states to identify workers who might serve on smallpox response teams to vaccinate others and provide critical services in the days following an attack. We are working with states to determine the exact number of individuals who will fall in these categories. To protect the American people the important thing is to ensure that we have health care workers and first responders ready to serve as smallpox response teams. However, we expect that some of the people identified by the states will not be eligible for vaccination because of a medical condition, and others may choose not to be vaccinated.

It has been reported that we will be vaccinating up to 10 million health care workers and first responders. However, we do not expect that the numbers of first responders and health care workers vaccinated in this part of the program to be that high.

The important thing is to ensure that we have health care workers and first responders ready to serve as smallpox response teams.

Are we less prepared to protect the American people if we don't get participation from millions of public health and health care workers or first responders?

Whatever the number of people who choose to participate and get vaccinated, we will be much more prepared to protect the American people than we are today.

Also, the very fact that states, hospitals and communities will have vaccination plans—for emergency responders and for mass-vaccinating the general public—makes us better prepared to protect Americans in an emergency.

These efforts will increase deterrence.

Will you administer tests to ensure that health care workers and first responders receiving the vaccine are not pregnant or HIV positive?

Every person volunteering to receive the vaccine will be asked detailed questions regarding their medical history and physical health and will be educated to the risks and possible side effects of the vaccine. If there is any indication that a person has a contraindication for the vaccine, the individual will be referred to the local public health department or another health care provider for testing.

How can a person protect against the risk of inadvertent transmission of the vaccine to another person?

Anyone receiving the vaccine will be instructed on several readily available steps to prevent the accidental transmission of the vaccine to another person. For example, the vaccinated person should use breathable bandages, wear a long-sleeve shirt, and use good hand hygiene.

How will the government monitor and report side effects?

The CDC is enlisting an outside group that will constitute an external data monitoring and safety review board. This external review board will review, in real time, vaccine adverse event reports and data, interpret findings, and provide guidance and advice for strengthening the overall safety of the program if needed.

How does this decision differ from the vaccination program in Israel? The vaccination program in the United Kingdom (U.K.)?

Israel is vaccinating health care workers and military personnel who were previously vaccinated. In the U.K., a small group of roughly 1000 people are being vaccinated.

Is it true that those who were vaccinated previously have a lower risk of adverse reaction?

Those who were vaccinated previously may have a lower risk of adverse reactions. It is appropriate for individuals, in deciding whether to be vaccinated, to consider whether they were vaccinated previously.

How will vaccine adverse events be handled? What protocols will be followed for actual or claimed serious adverse events?

Prospective vaccinees will be educated about the contraindications to smallpox vaccination in order to minimize serious adverse reactions to the vaccine. A good system to monitor and treat adverse events will be an integral part of this policy, and will be done in close collaboration between the CDC, states, and public health agencies and hospitals. The states will maintain records of people vaccinated and will work with hospitals to set up systems to diagnose, manage, and treat people who experience adverse reactions from the vaccine. This will include rapid access to the primary treatment for most serious adverse events, Vaccinia Immune Globulin (VIG).

It is expected that most of the side effects caused by smallpox vaccinations will not require special treatment or therapy. There are two treatments that may help people who have certain serious reactions to the smallpox vaccine. These are: Vaccinia Immune Globulin (VIG) and Cidofovir [an antiviral drug]. Patients receiving these drugs would need to stay in the hospital for observation and possible additional treatment, as the VIG and Cidofovir may cause a number of side effects as well. CDC will review summary reports of adverse events and will investigate all individual reports of serious events.

Vaccinating the public

What is the current threat assessment? Who are likely countries to obtain and use the virus?

Terrorists or governments hostile to the United States may have, or could obtain, some of the variola virus that causes smallpox disease. If so, these adversaries could use it as a biological weapon. This potential along with an appreciation for the potentially devastating consequences of a smallpox attack, suggests that we should take prudent steps to prepare our critical responders to protect the American public should an attack occur. People exposed to variola virus, or those at risk of being exposed, can be protected by vaccinia (smallpox) vaccine. The United States is taking precautions to deal with this possibility.

If a person wants to sign up to receive the vaccine as soon as possible, what should they do?

The federal government is not recommending that members of the general public be vaccinated at this point. Our government has no information that a biological attack is imminent, and there are significant side effects and risks associated with the vaccine. HHS is in the process of establishing an orderly process to make unlicensed vaccine available to those adult members of the general public without medical contraindications who insist on being vaccinated either in 2003, with an unlicensed vaccine, or in 2004, with a licensed vaccine. (A member of the general public may also be eligible to volunteer for an on-going clinical trial for next generation vaccines.)

The federal government is not recommending that members of the general public be vaccinated at this point.

How long will it take before HHS begins administering vaccines to the general public under the new program?

Again, we do not recommend at this point that the general public be vaccinated. However, we expect to be able to make the unlicensed vaccine available to those who insist on being vaccinated sometime in the spring of 2003. The immediate task for state and federal government will remain the implementation of our program to vaccinate our emergency responders. This is necessary to best protect Americans in the event of a release.

Of course, in the event of an actual attack, we will immediately make vaccine available to those at risk from disease.

Who will administer the vaccines?

State health departments, with guidance from CDC, will set up vaccination clinics and determine who will be staffing clinics and administering smallpox vaccine. The number of vaccination sites will be determined in the state plans, and depends in large part on the demand for the vaccines. CDC is assisting states with planning, technical assistance and education.

If you aren't recommending that the general public be vaccinated, why are you setting up this special program to allow them to get the vaccine?

We understand that some Americans will want to be vaccinated despite the risks. The President decided that the best course was to provide Americans with as much information as we can, help them weigh the risks, then let them decide for themselves. . . .

Vaccine safety

How safe is the smallpox vaccine?

The smallpox vaccine is the best protection you can get if you are exposed to the smallpox virus. Most people experience normal, usually mild, reactions, such as sore arm, fever, headache, body ache, and fatigue. These symptoms may peak eight to 12 days after vaccination.

In the past, about 1,000 people for every 1,000,000 (1 million) vaccinated people experienced reactions that were serious, but not life-threatening. Most involved spread of virus elsewhere on the body.

In the past, between 14 and 52 people out of 1,000,000 vaccinated for the first time experienced potentially life-threatening reactions. These reactions included serious skin reactions and inflammation of the brain (encephalitis). From past experience, one or two people in 1 million who receive smallpox vaccine may die as a result.

Serious side effects generally are rarer after revaccination, compared to first vaccinations.

Careful screening of potential vaccine recipients is essential to ensure that those at increased risk do not receive the vaccine.

People most likely to have side effects are people who have, or even once had, skin conditions, (especially eczema or atopic dermatitis) and people with weakened immune systems, such as those who have received a transplant, are HIV positive, or are receiving treatment for cancer. Anyone who falls within these categories, or lives with someone who falls into one of these categories, should NOT get the smallpox vaccine unless they are exposed, or at risk of exposure, to the disease. In addition, anyone who falls within the following categories should not get the smallpox vaccine unless they are exposed or at risk of exposure: pregnant women, breastfeeding mothers, anyone who is allergic to the vaccine or any of its components, and anyone under the age of 18.

So your estimate is that at least one person per million will die as a result of this vaccine?

This is a statistical estimate based on prior experience with the vaccine. However, we will work hard to prevent even these rare events from happening. Severe reactions can be minimized by screening people for bars to vaccination before vaccinating them and closely monitoring individuals for severe reactions with prompt treatment as necessary.

From past experience, one or two people in 1 million who receive smallpox vaccine may die as a result.

Is there any way to treat bad reactions to the vaccine?

Two treatments may help people who have certain serious reactions to the smallpox vaccine. These are Vaccinia Immune Globulin (VIG) and Cidofovir. We will have more than 2,700 treatment doses of VIG (enough for predicted reactions with more than 27 million people) at the end of December 2002, and 3,500 doses of Cidofovir (enough for predicted reactions with 15 million people).

Has the Food and Drug Administration (FDA) approved the use of 15 pricks to vaccinate both primary vaccinees and revacinees? If not, will this approval have come before the Department of Defense (DoD) begins to vaccinate troops? If it does not, will DoD be giving 15 pricks to 1st time vaccinees? (The current package insert states 3 pricks for primary vaccinees and 15 pricks for revaccinees).

CDC and others are currently in the process of submitting data to the FDA to support changing the recommendation of 3 needle sticks for primary vaccinations to 15 needle sticks for both primary and revaccination.

It is important to note that during the smallpox eradication period, the World Health Organization (WHO) program utilized 15 needle sticks universally to avoid confusion and to help decrease the number of vaccine take failures from flaws in vaccine administration techniques. However, until the FDA approves a package insert change, vaccinators should follow the instructions found on the vaccine package insert on the number of needle sticks to administer for primary vaccines and revaccinees.

What should I expect at the vaccination site?

If the vaccination is successful, a red and itchy bump develops at the vaccination site in three or four days. In the first week after vaccination, the bump becomes a large blister, fills with pus, and begins to drain. During week two, the blister begins to dry up and a scab forms. The scab falls off in the third week, leaving a small scar. People who are being vaccinated for the first time may have a stronger "take" (a successful reaction) than those who are being revaccinated. Most people experience normal, usually mild, reactions, such as sore arm, fever, headache, body ache, and fatigue. These symptoms may peak eight to 12 days after vaccination. The vaccine virus (vaccinia) is present on the skin at the vaccination site until the scab falls off. One must take care not to touch it so that the vaccine virus (vaccinia) is not spread elsewhere, especially to the eyes, nose, mouth, genitalia or rectum.

Are there any side effects of the vaccine?

Yes, side effects can result from smallpox vaccination. Mild reactions include swelling and tender lymph nodes that can last two to four weeks after the blister heals. Up to 20 percent of people develop headache, fatigue, muscle aches, pain, or chills after smallpox vaccination, usually about eight to 12 days later. Some individuals may have rashes that last two to four days. These side effects are usually temporary and self-limiting, meaning they go away on their own or with minimal medical treatment, for example aspirin and rest. . . .

Medical experts believe that with careful screening, monitoring and early intervention the number of serious adverse reactions can be minimized.

13

No One Should Be Vaccinated Against Smallpox

Todd Sloane

Todd Sloane is assistant managing editor of Modern Healthcare.

The U.S. government is asking health care providers to be vaccinated against smallpox so they will be protected in the event of a bioterror attack. This proposal seems foolish because there is little reason to believe that such an attack will occur. Vaccination is risky, both because people may have severe reactions to the vaccine and because vaccinated people can spread the disease to others. Furthermore, the government is not offering to pay for it, and its costs could force health care systems to suspend more useful programs. Nonetheless, few have protested the program because no one wants to seem to oppose "preparedness."

In late January 2003, healthcare providers will be subjected to a hugely expensive and risky public health experiment for no compelling reason and with only a murmur of dissent.

The smallpox vaccination program affecting hundreds of thousands of healthcare workers and millions of other Americans is to take place without a shred of evidence of a credible threat of a bioterror attack. The plan is nationwide, despite Al Qaeda's [the base, an Islamic terrorist group] predilection attacking high-profile targets in major urban areas where casualties would be greatest. The inoculation is risky, given the chances of adults getting sick or spreading the disease after getting a dose of this live vaccine. And Washington isn't offering to pay for it, leaving already shortchanged public health agencies and hospitals to cover the costs. In short, it's bad science, bad public policy and bad business, yet hardly anyone is saying anything against it.

Of course, we all know why. Most public health officials, hospital executives and physicians are afraid of appearing to be against "preparedness," that all-encompassing term that has taken on hues of red, white

Todd Sloane, "No Clear and Present Danger," *Modern Healthcare*, vol. 33, January 12, 2003, p. 20. Copyright © 2003 by Crain Communications Inc., 360 N. Michigan Ave., Chicago, IL 60601. Reproduced by permission.

and blue but no shades of gray. If the White House says we need to do something for preparedness—even injecting healthy patients with a potentially dangerous vaccine against a virus that was wiped out worldwide 32 years ago—we are supposed to take our orders and march, no questions asked.

[Bush's smallpox inoculation plan is] bad science, bad public policy and bad business.

Of course, if there were credible evidence the evildoers had the smallpox virus and the weaponry and means to deliver it to this country, I might go stand in line for the vaccine myself. But I also agree with Linda Rosenstock, a physician and dean of the University of California, Los Angeles (UCLA) School of Public Health, who wrote recently: "If the risk is dramatically close to zero, as many of us in the health field believe, then a prudent course would be to continue as we are doing: working rapidly to manufacture a safer vaccine than now exists, to be available when and if the risk determination changes."

Where is the risk?

The only risk I see is to the health workers getting the vaccine, but in the era of preparedness that seems to be of little concern. American Hospital Association officials told *Modern Healthcare* reporter Julie Piotrowski that the feds need to clarify the necessity of prevaccination tests to screen out at-risk healthcare workers, including those who are pregnant or may have HIV, and whether workers should stay home after being vaccinated to prevent secondary transmission of infections. A committee at the Centers for Disease Control and Prevention surprisingly recommended against both mandatory screening prior to vaccination and routine administrative leave. Given that the clinical work on exposure risk took place in the 1960s, that's a highly suspect recommendation.

The costs and the impact on providers of this misguided program can only be guessed. After the first phase of half a million civilian health and emergency workers being vaccinated, phase two calls for 10 million emergency medical technicians, firefighters, healthcare workers and police officers to be offered the vaccine. Public health officials aren't sure how they are going to pay for phase one, let alone phase two.

The Pueblo (Colorado) City and County Health Department may temporarily curtail standard immunization clinics for children to carry out the smallpox program. Maybe I don't have the same intelligence data as the Bushies do, but isn't there just a chance that the terrorists already have crossed rural Colorado off their target list?

I suppose there is an off-chance that the Bush administration has the evidence to justify its program, but until it's ready to share, I would follow the lead of the few healthcare providers who have been brave enough to just say no.

14

Scientific Research and Publication Should Be Restricted to Prevent Bioterrorism

John D. Steinbruner and Elisa D. Harris

John D. Steinbruner is director of the Center for International and Security Studies at Maryland (CISSM) and professor of public policy at the University of Maryland. Elisa D. Harris is a senior research scholar at CISSM and former director for nonproliferation and export controls on the National Security Council staff.

The anthrax attacks of fall 2001 showed that the threat of bioterrorism is real. Advances in biotechnology could make it far worse. Even research that is in itself well intentioned can be used for dangerous purposes, possibly producing disease-causing microorganisms that cannot be stopped by current vaccines or treatments. Because of these risks, the U.S. government needs not only to make acquisition of dangerous pathogens more difficult but also to restrict publication, and perhaps even conduct, of sensitive but unclassified research that could be used by bioterrorists. Similar oversight also needs to be implemented on a global level. A possible global oversight system, the Biological Research Security System, is outlined.

Remarkable advances are underway in the biological sciences. One can credibly imagine the eradication of a number of known diseases, but also the deliberate or inadvertent creation of new disease agents that are dramatically more dangerous than those that currently exist. Depending on how the same basic knowledge is applied, millions of lives might be enhanced, saved, degraded, or lost.

Unfortunately, this ability to alter basic life processes is not matched by a corresponding ability to understand or manage the potentially neg-

John D. Steinbruner and Elisa D. Harris, "Controlling Dangerous Pathogens," *Issues in Science and Technology*, vol. 19, Spring 2003, pp. 47–54. Copyright © 2003 by Issues in Science and Technology. Reproduced by permission.

ative consequences of such research. At the moment there is very little organized protection against the deliberate diversion of science to malicious purposes. There is even less protection against the problem of inadvertence, of legitimate scientists initiating chains of consequence they cannot visualize and did not intend.

Current regulation of advanced biology in the United States is concerned primarily with controlling access to dangerous pathogens. Only very limited efforts have been made thus far to consider the potential implications of proposed research projects before they are undertaken. Instead, attention is increasingly being directed toward security classification and expanded biodefense efforts to deal with concerns about the misuse of science for hostile purposes. Few U.S. officials appear to recognize the global scope of the microbiological research community, and thus the global nature of the threat. We believe that more systematic protection, based on internationally agreed rules, is necessary to prevent destructive applications of the biological sciences, and we have worked with colleagues to develop one possible approach.

The emerging threat

Shortly after the September 11, 2001, terrorist attacks, envelopes containing relatively pure, highly concentrated *Bacillus anthracis* powder were mailed to several prominent U.S. media outlets and politicians.

After years of warnings, anthrax had been unleashed in a bioterrorist attack on U.S. soil. In the end, 5 people died and 17 were injured. An estimated 32,000 people were given antibiotics prophylactically, with some 10,300 of those being urged to continue treatment for 60 days. Although adherence to the full treatment regimen was poor, the prompt initiation of antibiotics may have prevented hundreds if not thousands of others from dying or becoming ill. What would have happened if a more sophisticated delivery system or an antibiotic-resistant strain of anthrax had been used instead?

Biological weapons experts have debated for years whether the biotechnology revolution would lead to the development of new types of biological agents that were more lethal, more difficult to detect, or harder to treat. Some believed that there was little advantage in trying to improve the wide range of highly dangerous pathogens already available in nature. Beginning in the late 1980s, however, reports from defectors and other former Soviet biological weapons scientists proved this notion to be false. According to these sources, under the Soviet offensive program, *Legionella* bacteria were genetically engineered to produce myelin, resulting in an autoimmune disease with a mortality rate in animals of nearly 100 percent. In another project, Venezuelan equine encephalomyelitis genes were inserted into vaccinia (the vaccine strain of smallpox) reportedly as part of an effort to create new combination agents known as "chimeras." In yet another project, genes from a bacterium that causes food poisoning, *Bacillus cereus*, were introduced into *Bacillus anthracis*, producing a more virulent strain of anthrax that even killed hamsters that had been vaccinated against the disease.

One need not look only to the former Soviet program for examples of how advances in the biological sciences could be deliberately or inadvertently misused for destructive applications. Research with possible destructive consequences is also being carried out in the civilian biomedical and agricultural community, both in universities and private-sector laboratories. Perhaps the most famous example is the mousepox experiment, in which Australian researchers trying to develop a means of controlling the mouse population inserted an interleukin-4 (IL-4) gene into the mousepox virus and in so doing created a pathogen that was lethal even to mice vaccinated against the disease. This work immediately raised the question of whether the introduction of IL-4 into other orthopox viruses, such as smallpox, would have similarly lethal effects. It also drew attention to the absence of internationally agreed rules on how to handle research results that could be misused. After publication of the research in February 2001, Ian Ramshaw, one of the principal investigators, called for the creation of an international committee to provide advice to scientists whose research produces unexpectedly dangerous results.

Other research projects since that time have been equally controversial. In one Department of Defense (DOD)–funded study, published in *Science* in July 2002, researchers from the State University of New York at Stony Brook created an infectious poliovirus from scratch by using genomic information available on the Internet and custom-made DNA material purchased through the mail. Members of Congress responded with a resolution criticizing the journal for publishing what was described as a blueprint for terrorists to create pathogens for use against Americans and calling on the executive branch to review existing policies regarding the classification and publication of federally funded research. Craig Venter of the private human genome project described the poliovirus work as "irresponsible" and, with University of Pennsylvania ethicist Arthur Caplan, called for new mechanisms to review and approve similar projects before they are carried out. A few months later, Venter and Nobel laureate Hamilton O. Smith announced their own rather provocative research goal: the creation of a novel organism with the minimum number of genes necessary to sustain life. Although the researchers emphasized that the organism would be deliberately engineered to prevent it from causing disease in humans or surviving outside of a laboratory dish, they acknowledged that others could use the same techniques to create new types of biological warfare agents.

There is very little organized protection against the deliberate diversion of science to malicious purposes.

In another project, University of Pennsylvania researchers, using previously published data on smallpox DNA, reverse-engineered a smallpox protein from vaccinia and then showed how smallpox evades the human immune system. The research, published in June 2002, raised the question of whether the same protein could be used to make other orthopox viruses such as vaccinia more lethal. In an unusual move the article was accompanied by a commentary defending publication and arguing that it was more likely to stimulate advances in vaccines or viral therapy than to threaten security.

Researchers have also begun to discuss the implications of the progress made in recent years in sequencing the genome of the virus responsible for the 1918 influenza pandemic. In 1997, researchers at the Armed Forces Institute of Pathology succeeded in recovering fragments of the virus from preserved tissue samples. By spring 2003, several of the eight segments of the virus genome have been sequenced and published. Once the complete sequence is obtained, it may be possible to use reverse genetics to recreate the deadly virus, which is estimated to have killed as many as 40 million people in a single year.

Other, more future-oriented research is also of concern. Steven Block, who led a 1997 study for the U.S. government on next-generation biological weapons, has called attention to the possibility of gene therapy being subverted to introduce pathogenic sequences into humans, or of new zoonotic agents being developed that move from animals to humans. Both Block and George Poste, who chairs a DOD panel on biological weapons threats, have also noted the possibility of stealth viruses that could be introduced into a victim but not activated until later and of designer diseases that could disrupt critical body functions.

New restrictions

Thus far, the U.S. response to these developments has had a distinctly national focus. Less than a month after the first anthrax death, Congress enacted legislation aimed at tightening access to pathogens and other dual-use biological materials within the United States. Under the USA Patriot Act, signed into law on October 26, 2001, it is a crime for anyone to knowingly possess any biological agent, toxin, or delivery system that is not reasonably justified for prophylactic, protective bona fide research or other peaceful purposes. The bill also makes it a crime for certain restricted person, including illegal aliens and individuals from terrorist list countries, to possess, transport, or receive any of the threat agents on the Centers for Disease Control and Prevention's (CDC's) "select agents" list. The American Society for Microbiology (ASM) and others have criticized the restricted-persons provision, arguing that the absence of waiver authority could preclude legitimate researchers from restricted countries from undertaking work that could benefit the United States.

Other bioterrorism legislation passed in May 2002 requires any person who possesses, uses, or transfers a select agent to register with the secretary of Health and Human Services (HHS) and to adhere to safety and security requirements commensurate with the degree of risk that each agent poses to public health. The law requires a government background check for anyone who is to be given access to select agents. In addition, HHS is required to develop a national database of registered persons and the select agents they possess, including strain and other characterizing information if available, and to carry out inspections of relevant facilities. The Department of Agriculture (USDA) is required to develop parallel registration, security, record-keeping, and inspection measures for facilities that transfer or possess certain plant and animal pathogens. These new controls build on legislation adapted in 1996, after the Oklahoma City bombings and the acquisition of plague cultures by a member of the Aryan Nation, requiring any person involved in the transfer of a select agent to register with HHS and notify it of all proposed transfers.

In another move, seemingly at odds with the greatly expanded effort to control access to dangerous pathogens, the government has dramatically increased research funding related to biological warfare agents. In March 2002, the National Institutes of Health (NIH) announced a $1.7 billion fiscal year 2003 bioterrorism research program, a 2,000 percent increase over pre–September 11 budget levels. Under the program, some $440 million is to be spent on basic research, including genomic sequencing and proteomic analysis of up to 25 pathogens, and $520 million is to be used for new high-containment and maximum-containment laboratories and regional centers for bioterrorism training and research. In his 2003 State of the Union message, President George W. Bush proposed to spend an additional $6 billion over 10 years to develop and quickly make available biological warfare agent vaccines and treatments under a new HHS-Department of Homeland Security program called Project Bioshield. The Department of Energy (DOE) has also been increasing its bioterrorism research program, which was first begun in 1997. As part of this effort, DOE is funding research aimed at determining the complete genetic sequence of anthrax and other potential biological warfare agents and comparing agent strains and species using DNA information. Other DOE studies are using genetic sequencing to identify genes that influence virulence and antibiotic resistance in anthrax and plague and to determine the structure of the lethal toxins produced by botulinum and other biological agents that can be used against humans.

Against this backdrop of increased research, the United States is also exploring possible restrictions on the dissemination of scientific findings that could have national security implications—what has been called "sensitive but unclassified" information. Since the Ronald Reagan administration, U.S. policy on this issue has been enshrined in National Security Decision Directive (NSDD) 189, which states: ". . . to the maximum extent possible, the products of fundamental research [should] remain unrestricted . . . where the national security requires control, the mechanism for control of information generated during federally funded fundamental research in science, technology and engineering . . . is classification." National Security Advisor Condoleezza Rice affirmed the administration's commitment to NSDD 189 in a November 2001 letter.

Stealth viruses . . . could be introduced into a victim but not activated until later.

But in a memorandum to federal agencies in March 2002, White House Chief of Staff Andrew Card raised the need to protect sensitive but unclassified information. At the same time, the Pentagon circulated a draft directive containing proposals for new categories of controlled information and for prepublication review of certain DOD-funded research. Because of strong criticism from the scientific community, the draft was withdrawn. In fall 2002, however, the White House Office of Management and Budget began developing rules for the "discussion and publication" of information that could have national security implications.

These rules, which were reportedly requested by Homeland Security chief Tom Ridge, are expected to apply to research conducted by government scientists and contractors but not, at least initially, to federally funded research grants. This has not assuaged the concerns of the 42,000-member ASM, which in July 2002 sent a letter to the National Academies asking it to convene a meeting with journal publishers to explore measures the journals could implement voluntarily as an alternative to government regulation. This meeting, which was held in January 2003, laid the groundwork for a subsequent decision by 30 journal editors and scientists to support the development of new processes for considering the national security implications of proposed manuscripts and, where necessary, to modify or refrain from publishing papers whose potential harm outweighs their potential societal benefits.

The government has . . . taken a very modest step toward strengthening the oversight process for biotechnology research in the United States.

In a surprising move, the government has also taken a very modest step toward strengthening the oversight process for biotechnology research in the United States. Under the new HHS regulations to implement the May 2002 controls on the possession, transfer, and use of select agents, the HHS secretary must approve genetic engineering experiments that could make a select agent resistant to known drugs or otherwise more lethal. The new USDA regulations appear to be even broader, in that they seem to apply to any microorganism or toxin, not just to those on the USDA control list. The latter provision mirrors the current requirements of the NIH Guidelines, under which biotechnology research has been regulated for more than a quarter century.

Under the original NIH Guidelines, published by the NIH Recombinant DNA Advisory Committee (RAC) in 1976, six types of experiments were prohibited. However, once it became clear that recombinant DNA research could be conducted safely, without an adverse impact on public health or the environment, these prohibitions were replaced by a system of tiered oversight and review, in which Institutional Biosafety Committees (IBCs) and Institutional Review Boards (IRBs) at individual facilities replaced the RAC as the primary oversight authority for most categories of regulated research.

In 2003, only two categories of laboratory research involving recombinant DNA technology are subject to NIH oversight. The first, "major actions," cannot be initiated without the submission of relevant reformation on the proposed experiment to the NIH Office of Biotechnology Activities (OBA), and they require IBC approval, RAC review, and NIH director approval before initiation. This covers experiments that involve the "deliberate transfer of a drug resistance trait to microorganisms that are not known to acquire the trait naturally if such acquisition could compromise the use of the drug to control disease agents in humans, veterinary medicine, or agriculture." The second category of experiments requiring IBC approval and NIH/OBA review before initiation involves the cloning of toxin molecules with a median lethal dose (the dose found to be lethal to 50 percent of those to which it is administered) of less than 100 nanograms per kilogram of body weight. Unlike the requirements in the new select agent rules, the NIH Guidelines apply only to research conducted at institutes in the United States and abroad that received NIH funding for recombinant DNA research. Many private companies are believed to follow the guidelines voluntarily.

In addition to requiring prior approval for these two types of experiments, HHS and USDA asked for input from the scientific community on other types of experiments that might require enhanced oversight because of safety concerns, as well as on the form that such additional oversight should take. In particular, they sought comments on experiments with biological agents that could increase their virulence or pathogenicity; change their natural mode of transmission, route of exposure, or host range in ways adverse to humans, animals, or plants; result in the deliberate transfer of a drug-resistant trait or a toxin-producing capability to a microorganism in a manner that does not involve recombinant DNA techniques; or involve the smallpox virus.

Interestingly, the ASM did not rule out the possible need for additional oversight of certain types of microbiological research. However, in its comments on the draft HHS regulations, the ASM recommended that any additional oversight requirements be implemented through the NIH Guidelines rather than regulations, in order to provide a less cumbersome means of incorporating changes as technology evolves. The ASM also proposed the creation of a Select Agent Research Advisory Committee to provide advice to U.S. government agencies, including reviewing specific research projects or categories of research for which additional oversight is required.

Any oversight system must be designed and operated primarily by scientists.

A number of the domestic measures described above were also incorporated in the U.S. proposal to the Biological Weapons Convention (BWC) review conference in October 2001. Three months earlier, the United States had rejected the legally binding protocol that had been under negotiation to strengthen the 1972 treaty's prohibition on the development, production, and possession of biological agents. In its place, the United States suggested a variety of largely voluntary measures to be pursued on a national basis by individual countries. This included a proposal that other countries adopt legislation requiring entities that possessed dangerous pathogens to register with the government, as is being done in the United States. The United States also proposed that countries implement strict biosafety procedures based on World Health Organization (WHO) or equivalent national guidelines, tightly regulate access to dangerous pathogens, explore options for national oversight of high-risk biological experiments, develop a code of conduct for scientists working with pathogens, and report internationally any biological releases that could affect other countries adversely. After an acrimonious meeting, which was suspended for a year after the U.S. call for the termination of both the protocol negotiations and the body in which they were being held, it was agreed that experts would meet for a two-week period each year to discuss five specific issues. Most of the issues related to strengthening controls over pathogens will be considered at the first experts' meeting, to be held in August 2003.

U.S. approach falls short

The early 2000s have thus witnessed a range of U.S. initiatives aimed at reducing the likelihood that advances in the biological sciences will be used for destructive purposes. But whether viewed as a whole or as a series of discrete steps, the current approach falls short in a number of important respects:

The new controls on human, plant, and animal pathogens are too narrowly focused on a static list of threat agents. These controls can be circumvented entirely by research such as the poliovirus experiment, which demonstrated a means of acquiring a controlled agent covertly, without the use of pathogenic material; or like the mousepox experiment, which showed how to make a relatively benign pathogen into something much more lethal.

The expanded bioterrorism research effort is rapidly increasing the number of researchers and facilities working with the very pathogens that U.S. policy is seeking to control, before appropriate oversight procedures for such research have been put into place. Little thought appears to have been given to the fact that the same techniques that provide insights into enhancing our defenses against biological agents can also be misused to develop even more lethal agents.

The proposed restrictions on sensitive but unclassified research will not prevent similar research from being undertaken and published in other countries. Depending on the form such restrictions take, they could also increase suspicions abroad about U.S. activities, impede oversight of research, and interfere with the normal scientific process through which researchers review, replicate, and refine each other's work and build on each other's discoveries.

The new oversight requirements for certain categories of biotechnology research, like the NIH Guidelines on which they are based, subject only a very narrow subset of relevant research to national-level review. And if the ASM proposal to implement these and other additional oversight requirements through the NIH Guidelines is accepted, these requirements will no longer have the force of law, unlike requirements contained in regulations.

Finally, because of the current U.S. antipathy toward legally binding multilateral agreements, the BWC experts' discussions on pathogen controls are unlikely to result in the adoption of a common set of standards for research that could have truly global implications.

As the mousepox experiment showed, advanced microbiological research is occurring in countries other than the United States. According to the chairman of the ASM Publications Board, of the nearly 14,000 manuscripts submitted to ASM's 11 peer-reviewed journals during 2002, about 60 percent included non-U.S. authors, from at least 100 different countries. A total of 224 of these manuscripts involved select agents, of which 115, or slightly more than half, had non-U.S. authors. Research regulations that apply only in the United States therefore will not only be ineffective but will put U.S. scientists at a competitive disadvantage. The need for uniform standards, embodied in internationally agreed rules, is abundantly clear.

In order to be effective and to be accepted by those most directly affected, a new oversight arrangement must, in addition to being global in scope, also achieve a number of other objectives. First, it must be bottom-up. Rather than being the result of a political process, like the select agent regulations or the proposed U.S. government publication restrictions, any oversight system must be designed and operated primarily by scientists those that have the technical expertise to make the necessary judgments about the potential implications of a given experiment.

Second, the system must be focused. It must define the obligations of individual scientists precisely in order to avoid uncertainty as to what is required to comply with agreed rules. This means relying on objective criteria rather than assessments of intent. This is especially important if the oversight system is legally binding, with possible penalties for violators. It also must be as limited as possible in terms of the range of activities that are covered. Not all microbiological research can or should be subject to oversight. Only the very small fraction of research that could have destructive applications is relevant.

Common standards, reflected in internationally agreed rules, are essential if the full promise of the biotechnology revolution is to be realized and potentially dangerous consequences minimized.

Third, it must be flexible. Like the NIH Guidelines, any new oversight arrangement must include a mechanism for adapting to technological change. Most current concerns revolve around pathogens—either the modification of existing pathogens or the creation of new pathogens that are more deadly than those that presently exist. But as Steven Block has noted, "black biology" will in the not-too-distant future lead to the development of compounds that can affect the immune system and other basic life systems, or of microorganisms that can invade a host and unleash their deadly poison before being detected.

Finally, any new oversight arrangement must be secure. Both the genetic modification work undertaken as part of the Soviet offensive program and the more recent U.S. biodefense efforts underscore the importance of including all three relevant research communities—government, industry, and academia—in any future oversight system. This will require the development of provisions that allow the necessary degree of independent review without, at the same time, jeopardizing government national security information or industry or academic proprietary interests.

What, then, might an internationally agreed oversight system aimed at achieving these objectives look like? To help explore this question, the Center for International and Security Studies at Maryland (CISSM) has, as part of a project launched even before September 11 and the anthrax attacks, consulted extensively with a diverse group of scientists, public policy experts, information technology specialists, and lawyers. Out of these deliberations has emerged a prototype system for protective oversight of certain categories of high-consequence biotechnology research. To the maximum extent possible, we have drawn on key elements of the oversight arrangements already in place. Like the NIH Guidelines, our system is based on the concept of tiered peer review, in which the level of risk of a particular research activity determines the nature and extent of oversight requirements. Like the select agent regulations, our system also includes provisions for registration (or licensing), reporting, and inspections.

We call our prototype the Biological Research Security System. At its foundation is a local review mechanism, or what we term a Local Pathogens Research Committee. This body is analogous to the IBCs and IRBs at universities and elsewhere in the United States that currently oversee recombinant DNA research (under the NIH Guidelines) and human clinical trials (under Food and Drug Administration regulations). In our system, this local committee would be responsible for overseeing potentially dangerous activities: research that increases the potential for otherwise benign pathogens to be used as weapons or that demonstrates techniques that could have destructive applications. This could include research that increases the virulence of a pathogen or that involves the *de novo* ("from scratch") synthesis of a pathogen, as was done in the poliovirus experiment. Oversight at this level would be exercised through a combination of personnel and facility licensing, project review, and where appropriate, project approval. Under our approach, the vast majority of microbiological research would either fall into this category or not be covered at all.

At the next level, there would be a national review body, which we call a National Pathogens Research Authority. This body is analogous to the RAC. It would be responsible for overseeing moderately dangerous activities: research involving controlled agents or related agents, especially experiments that increase the weaponization potential of such agents. This could include research that increases the transmissibility or environmental stability of a controlled agent, or that involves the production of such an agent in powder or aerosol form, which are the most common means of disseminating biological warfare agents. All projects that fall into this category would have to be approved at the national level and could be carried out only by licensed researchers at licensed facilities. The national body would also be responsible for overseeing the work of the local review committees, including licensing qualified researchers and facilities, and for facilitating communications between the local and international levels.

At the top of the system would be a global standard-setting and review body, which we term the International Pathogens Research Agency. The closest analogy to this is the WHO Advisory Committee on Variola Virus Research, which oversees research with the smallpox virus at the two WHO-approved depositories: the CDC in Atlanta and Vector in Russia. This new body would be responsible for overseeing and approving extremely dangerous activities: research largely involving the most dangerous controlled agents, including research that could make such agents even more dangerous. This could include work with an eradicated agent such as smallpox or the construction of an antibiotic- or vaccine-resistant controlled agent, as was done during the Soviet offensive program. All projects in this category would have to be approved internationally, as would the researchers and facilities involved.

In addition to overseeing extremely dangerous research, the global body would also be responsible for defining the research activities that would be subject to oversight under the different categories and overseeing implementation by national government of internationally agreed rules, including administering a secure database of information on research covered by the system. It would also help national governments in meeting their international obligations by, for example, providing assistance related to good laboratory practices. No existing organization currently fulfills all of these functions.

A more robust system

In today's climate of heightened concern about bioterrorism, the idea of building on existing oversight processes to put in place a more robust system of independent peer review of high-consequence research seems less radical than when CISSM began this project in 2001. In the United States, there is a growing awareness that current domestic regulations do not provide adequate protection against the use of biotechnology research for destructive purposes. In May 2002, a senior White House Office of Homeland Security official urged the scientific community to "define appropriate criteria and procedures" for regulating scientific research related to weapons of mass destruction. In late 2003, a special committee appointed by the National Academies will decide whether to recommend enhanced oversight of recombinant DNA research in the United States, above and beyond that currently regulated by the RAC.

Others are ahead of the United States in recognizing the global dimensions of the problem. In September 2002, the International Committee of the Red Cross called on governments, the scientific and medical communities, and industry to work together to ensure that there are "effective controls" over potentially dangerous biotechnology, biological research, and biological agents. And in the run-up to the continuation of the BWC review conference in fall 2002, the British counterpart to the National Academies, the Royal Society, called for agreement on a "universal set of standards for research" for incorporation into internationally supported treaties.

Thoughtful individuals will disagree about the research activities that should be covered by a new oversight arrangement, as well as the appropriate level of oversight that should be applied. They will also debate whether such a system should be legally binding, as envisioned in the prototype being developed by CISSM, or of a more voluntary nature, as has been suggested by researchers at Johns Hopkins University. But with each report of yet another high-consequence research project, fewer and fewer will doubt the nature of the emerging threat. Enhanced oversight of U.S. research is necessary but not sufficient. Common standards, reflected in internationally agreed rules, are essential if the full promise of the biotechnology revolution is to be realized and potentially dangerous consequences minimized. Our approach is one possible way of achieving that important goal.

15

Scientific Research and Publication Should Not Be Restricted

Abigail Salyers

Abigail Salyers is president of the American Society of Microbiology.

Frightening as the prospect of a bioterrorist attack is, it is important not to overreact. No restrictions should be placed on the conduct or publication of unclassified scientific research because open communication of research results is vital for the advance of science and the improvement of public health. Impeding the flow of scientific information is likely to harm rather than help efforts to prevent bioterrorism.

In the aftermath of the fall 2001 bioterrorism attacks, the wisdom of imposing restrictions on scientific publications has been widely discussed in the U.S. press. Debate about U.S. security interests and scientific communication is timely and worthwhile. It is critical, however, that we not overreact to these issues, especially if that overreaction puts scientific progress and the public health at even greater risk in any future bioterrorist action.

U.S. policy stipulates that no restriction may be placed on the conduct or reporting of federally funded unclassified research. Communication of research results forms a foundation for rapid and effective response to infectious diseases as well as to bioterrorism. The development of so many life-saving and life-improving therapeutics, including antibiotics and vaccines, has been possible because researchers can exchange information freely.

Censorship of scientific communication would provide a false sense of protection. For example, deleting methods sections from scientific publications, with the rationale that a terrorist could benefit from knowing the methodology, would certainly compromise our ability to replicate results, one of the cornerstones of scientific research. Scientific colleagues' scrutiny

Abigail Salyers, "Science, Censorship and Public Health," *Science*, vol. 296, April 26, 2002, p. 617.
Copyright © 2002 by AAAS. Reproduced by permission.

and replication of research studies reduces the likelihood of errors that can misdirect scientific activities.

Moreover, such secrecy could also increase the risks faced by the public. For example, lack of access to knowledge about the infectious capability of a small number of anthrax spores treated with anti-clumping agents contributed to the delay in responding effectively to the earliest cases of inhalation anthrax in fall 2001.

Open communication is the best protection

The best protection against the possibility of future bioterrorism incidents is the unfettered ability of our scientific community to collaborate openly and move forward rapidly in the conduct of scientific research. Timely communication of new knowledge and technological innovation accelerates the rate of scientific progress. For example, the rapidly accumulating new information from microbial genome sequences points toward new targets for therapeutic agents. With open access to these sequences, scientists can now translate the information into products that benefit human health.

Although scientists themselves are well aware of the importance of the free exchange of information within the research community, a community that transcends national boundaries, the public may not necessarily be convinced that scientists can be busted to this extent. There remains an undercurrent of public discomfort with what is seen by some, however wrongly, as freedom without responsibility. This generalized discomfort has been evident during the debates on the safety of genetically modified foods and the ethics of stem cell research.

Placing major new barriers in the path of the free flow of scientific information will ultimately undermine our best defenses against bioterrorism.

All of us in the scientific community, either individually or through our professional societies, must be prepared to make a strong and well-documented case for the importance of the free flow of information if such a defense becomes necessary. It is no longer sufficient to tell the public: "Trust us, we know what is good for you." We need to be able to explain why our position is in the public interest.

Terrorism feeds on fear, and fear feeds on ignorance. Our need to know the potential risks and consequences associated with bioterrorism agents is vital to the development of effective measures to ensure public safety. Placing major new barriers in the path of the free flow of scientific information will ultimately undermine our best defenses against bioterrorism and, ironically, compromise the public health that we are trying to protect.

Glossary

aerosolized: Made into particles or droplets small enough to be suspended in air, where they can be breathed in.

agroterrorism: Terrorist acts aimed at disrupting agriculture, for instance, introducing infectious plant or animal diseases.

animal husbandry: Care and raising of farm animals such as cattle and pigs.

anthrax: A disease of humans and animals caused by a bacterium, *Bacillus anthracis*, it has been used in one bioterrorist attack and is a candidate for others. It occurs in a cutaneous form spread by skin contact with spores of the bacterium, and an inhalational form spread by breathing the spores.

atopic dermatitis: Skin redness and itching caused by an allergy.

Aum Shinrikyo: A Japanese religious cult responsible for a nerve gas (sarin) attack in a Tokyo subway in 1995 that killed twelve people. The group had also attempted unsuccessfully to carry out bioterrorism attacks.

Bacillus anthracis: The bacterium that causes anthrax.

Biological and Toxin Weapons Convention: An international agreement made in 1972 to ban the development, production, stockpiling, and transfer of disease-causing microorganisms and natural poisons as weapons. It lacks measures to ensure treaty compliance, and the United States has refused to ratify it.

bioterrorism: Acts that create terror by deliberate introduction of living agents that cause disease.

botulism: A disease caused by bacteria that produce a powerful toxin (poison); usually spread naturally through food but might be usable as a bioterrorist weapon.

bovine spongiform encephalopathy: A fatal brain disease of cattle, spread (including possibly to humans) by eating nervous tissue of infected animals; popularly known as "mad cow disease."

CDC: The Centers for Disease Control and Prevention, the federal government's chief agency for tracking and controlling disease epidemics.

cidofovir: A new antiviral drug that may be effective against the smallpox virus.

Cipro: Trade name for ciprofloxacin, an antibiotic that can effectively treat anthrax.

contagious: Capable of being spread by direct or indirect contact.

contraindication: A reason not to perform a medical treatment on a person because it would cause harm; for example, because the person is allergic to some element of the treatment.

culling: Selecting certain members of a group, such as infected animals within a herd, so that they may be destroyed.

cultivar: A variety of a plant species originating and continuing in cultivation.

culture: A colony of microorganisms grown in a nutritive broth or solid.

dysentery: Intestinal disease, often caused by bacteria, marked by abdominal pain and severe diarrhea.

Ebola: A deadly disease caused by a virus, characterized by fever and extensive bleeding; a possible bioterror weapon.

eczema: A skin disease marked by redness, scaliness, and itching; people with this condition are advised not to take the smallpox vaccine.

endemic disease: A disease that is constantly present in a region but usually is more or less under control.

epidemic disease: A disease that spreads rapidly among many members of a community in a short period of time.

epidemiology: The study of the way disease spreads in a population and the reasons it occurs or does not occur in particular populations.

first responders: Those likely to be the first to attempt to control a disaster, such as health care workers, firefighters, and police officers.

foot-and-mouth disease: A serious and highly contagious virus-caused disease primarily of cattle and pigs. It can also infect sheep, deer, and other cloven-hoofed animals.

genomics: The study of the genomes, or complete collections of genes, of living things and the ways that genes interact.

hemorrhagic fever: One of several illnesses caused by viruses, marked by bleeding throughout the body and often fatal. Ebola and Marburg fevers are examples. The viruses that cause these diseases might be used as biological weapons.

HHS: The U.S. Department of Health and Human Services.

HIV: Human immunodeficiency virus, the virus usually held to be the cause of AIDS

iatrogenic: Caused by medical treatment.

indigenous: Native to a certain area.

infectious: Caused by a parasitic microorganism, or containing microorganisms that can cause disease.

infrastructure: The underlying structure (technology, personnel, etc.) that supports a system. For example, the infrastructure of a health care system includes workers, laboratory equipment, and information systems.

Legionella: The type of bacteria that causes Legionnaires' disease, a severe lung infection.

lesion: A sore or wound.

lymph nodes: Clusters of cells throughout the body that collect and destroy invading microorganisms and make cells that circulate in the immune system.

mad cow disease: Popular name for bovine spongiform encephalopathy.

monoculture: Raising only a single kind of crop plant, rather than using farmland for mixed crops or purposes.

multifocal: Occurring in several places at the same time.

myelin: A fatty material that makes a sheath around some nerves and is essential for their function.

nanotechnology: A process of creating microscopic machines by manipulating atoms and molecules.

outbreak: A sudden occurrence of disease.

palliative care: Care that increases a sick person's comfort but does not attempt to cure the illness.

pandemic: An epidemic that affects a large part of the world at about the same time.

pathogen: Any organism, especially a microorganism, that can cause disease.

prophylaxis: A treatment that prevents or protects against disease.

proteomic: Related to the structure and function of proteins (a major class of biochemicals) and their manufacture by genes.

protocol: A formal plan or set of procedures to be followed during a scientific experiment or course of medical treatment.

quarantine: Separation of infected from uninfected individuals in order to prevent the spread of contagious disease.

Rajneeshees: Members of a cult devoted to guru Bhagwan Shree Rajneesh. In 1984 a Rajneeshee group staging poisoned salad bars in an Oregon town with salmonella, staging the only successful bioterrorism attack in the United States prior to the fall 2001 anthrax attacks.

ring containment: A procedure for controlling a disease outbreak after it has begun by vaccinating all those exposed to the disease, then all their contacts (family, friends, coworkers), the contacts of those contacts, and so on.

salmonella: A group of bacteria that cause digestive illnesses, some of which can cause death. They are usually spread through food or water.

smallpox: A serious disease that can cause blindness, disfigurement, or death, caused by a virus (variola); natural smallpox was eradicated worldwide in the late 1970s, but stocks of the virus remain and may be used as a bioterror weapon.

spores: Hardy forms taken on by some bacteria (such as the one that causes anthrax), fungi, and other organisms that help in the survival and spread of those organisms.

surge capability: The power to handle a sudden increase in demand for services, such as demands on a health care system made by an epidemic.

symptom: A sign of disease, such as fever or a cough.

syndromic surveillance: Looking for disease outbreaks (including those caused by bioterror) by watching for unusual increases in the number of people reporting particular groups of symptoms or buying medicine to treat such symptoms.

telemedicine: Medicine performed at a distance with the aid of computers and communication devices.

toxin: A poison made naturally by a living thing, such as a microorganism.

tularemia: Rabbit fever, an infectious disease of rodents and rabbits caused by a bacterium. It can be transmitted to humans and is a possible bioterror agent.

vaccinia: The virus that causes cowpox, a usually mild disease; vaccinia is closely related to the smallpox virus and is used in the vaccine against smallpox.

virulent: Able to cause serious, rapidly advancing disease.

West Nile virus: A virus originally found in birds that can also infect and sometimes cause serious disease in humans; outbreaks of this disease were first detected in the United States in 1999.

Yersinia pestis: The bacterium that causes bubonic and pneumonic plague.

zoonotic disease: A disease of vertebrate animals that can be transmitted to humans.

Organizations and Websites

The editors have compiled the following list of organizations concerned with the issues debated in this book. The descriptions are derived from materials provided by the organizations. All have publications or information available for interested readers. The list was compiled on the date of publication of the present volume; the information provided here may change. Be aware that many organizations take several weeks or longer to respond to inquiries, so allow as much time as possible.

ANSER Institute for Homeland Security
2900 South Quincy St., Suite 800, Arlington, VA 22206
(703) 416-3597
e-mail: homelandsecurity@anser.org • website: www.homelandsecurity.org

ANSER (Analytical Services, Inc.), a nonprofit public service research corporation, provides research to the military and government agencies. Its Institute of Homeland Security was established in April 2001 to do research and provide executive education and public awareness regarding challenges to the nation's security in the twenty-first century. The institute's website includes information on Dark Winter, a simulation of a smallpox bioterror attack on the United States conducted in winter 2002; an assessment of the biological weapons threat to the United States; and a proposal for protecting the food supply from bioterrorist attacks.

Cato Institute
1000 Massachusetts Ave. NW, Washington, DC 20001-5403
(202) 842-0200
website: www.cato.org

Founded in 1977, the Cato Institute is a nonprofit public policy research organization foundation. It supports the principles of limited government, individual liberty, free markets, and peace. Its website includes publications on bioterrorism.

Center for Civilian Biodefense Strategies
Center for Biosecurity, University of Pittsburgh Medical Center
200 Lathrop St., Pittsburgh, PA 15213-2582
(800) 533-8762
e-mail: upmcweb@upmc.edu • website: www.upmc-biosecurity.org

The center, formerly part of Johns Hopkins University's Bloomberg School of Public Health, became affiliated with the Center for Biosecurity of the University of Pittsburgh Medical Center in November 2003. It is an independent, nonprofit organization that works to prevent the development and use of biological weapons and to lessen their effectiveness and the human suffering that might result from them. It publishes a magazine called *Biosecurity and Bioterrorism*. Its website includes publications such as *The Challenge of Hospital Infection During a Response to Bioterrorist Attack* and *Biodefense R&D: Anticipating Future Threats, Establishing a Strategic Environment*.

118

Center for the Study of Bioterrorism
3545 Lafayette Ave., Suite 300, St. Louis, MO 63104
(314) 977-8257
website: www.bioterrorism.slu.edu

This academic research center is part of the Saint Louis University School of Public Health. Its website includes references, news, links to Internet resources, online journal articles, and accounts of research. Material there covers specific pathogens such as anthrax, smallpox, and plague as well as contact information and emergency procedures.

Centers for Disease Control and Prevention (CDC)
Public Inquiry c/o BPRP
Bioterrorism Preparedness and Response Planning
Mailstop C-18
1600 Clifton Rd., Atlanta, GA 30333
e-mail: cdcresponse@ashastd.org • website: www.bt.cdc.gov

The CDC, part of the U.S. Department of Health and Human Services, is the government agency charged with protecting the public health of the nation by preventing and controlling diseases and by responding to public health emergencies. The CDC Emergency Preparedness and Response website discusses specific disease agents, such as smallpox and anthrax, that might be used in a bioterror attack; contains news related to bioterrorism protection; and includes links to pages describing preparedness programs and whom to contact in an emergency.

Council on Foreign Relations
1779 Massachusetts Ave. NW, Washington, DC 20036
(202) 518-3400 • fax: (202) 986-2984
e-mail: communications@cfr.org • website: http://cfrterrorism.org

The council is a nonpartisan membership organization, research center, and publisher. It is dedicated to increasing America's understanding of the world and contributing ideas to U.S. foreign policy. It publishes the magazine *Foreign Affairs*. Its online "terrorism encyclopedia" includes Q&A fact sheets such as "Responding to Biological Attacks," "Smallpox," and "Food and Agriculture."

National Institute of Allergy and Infectious Diseases
31 Center Dr., MSC 2520, Room 7A-50, Bethesda, MD 20892-2520
website: www.niaid.nih.gov/biodefense

The National Institute of Allergy and Infectious Diseases is the part of the National Institutes of Health that handles research on infectious diseases, including those that might be spread by bioterrorists. Its Biodefense Research website includes news, descriptions of research projects, and links to fact sheets and overviews related to bioterrorism prevention and response, such as a summary of NIAID accomplishments in biodefense research, a description of Project Bioshield, and comprehensive information on smallpox and the government's smallpox vaccination plan.

U.S. Department of Defense
Directorate of Public Inquiry and Analysis
Office of the Secretary of Defense (Public Affairs)
The Pentagon, Room 3A750, 14 Defense Pentagon
Washington, DC 20301-1400
website: www.defenselink.mil

The Department of Defense is responsible for the defense of the United States. Its website includes news stories about bioterrorism.

U.S. Department of Health and Human Services (HHS)
200 Independence Ave. SW, Washington, DC 20201
toll free: (877) 696-6775
website: www.hhs.gov

The U.S. Department of Health and Human Services deals with all health and welfare issues, including health and medical care for particular populations (such as the elderly and children), disease prevention, research on particular diseases, and preparation for disasters, including bioterrorism attacks. The website has links to several government sites that contain information about bioterrorism as well as specific documents related to bioterrorism, such as "Countering Bioterrorism and Other Threats to the Food Supply" and "Investigation of Bioterrorism-Related Anthrax and Interim Guidelines for Exposure Management."

U.S. Food and Drug Administration (FDA)
5600 Fishers Ln., Rockville, MD 20857
toll free: (888) 463-6332
website: www.fda.gov

The FDA is the federal government agency responsible for guaranteeing the safety of food, drugs, and cosmetics. Its counterterrorism website includes publications on countering bioterrorism, biological agents, advice for citizens on bioterrorism issues, and countering threats to the food supply.

Websites

National Library of Medicine, MEDLINEplus
www.nlm.nih.gov

MEDLINEplus is an online service of the National Library of Medicine, part of the National Institutes of Health, that provides links to health information for consumers. This page contains links to news stories and overviews related to bioterrorism, including specific agents such as anthrax and smallpox, methods of coping with an attack, and ways to prevent or treat an attack.

New Scientist
www.newscientist.com

This academic magazine's "hot topics" site on bioterrorism includes special reports on bioterrorism and bioweapons, including breaking news, bioterrorism risks, biodefense, smallpox, anthrax, and bioweapons treaties.

Terrorism Research Center, Inc.
www.terrorism.com

The Terrorism Research Center, founded in 1996, is an independent institute that conducts research on terrorism, homeland security, and related topics. They have asked that students not contact them, but their website contains considerable links and material on terrorism, including links to sites related to bioterrorism.

Bibliography

Books

Yonah Alexander and Milton M. Hoenig	*Super Terrorism: Biological, Chemical, and Nuclear.* Ardsley, NY: Transnational, 2001.
John G. Bartlett et al., eds.	*Bioterrorism and Public Health: An Internet Resource Guide.* Montvale, NJ: Thomson Medical Economics, 2002.
Raghav N. Bhatnagar	*Understanding Bioterrorism.* Baltimore, MD: American Literary Press, 2002.
W. Seth Carus	*Bioterrorism and Biocrimes: The Illicit Use of Biological Agents Since 1900.* Washington, DC: Center for Counterproliferation Research, National Defense University, 2002.
Eric Croddy, Clarisa Perez-Armendariz, and John Hart	*Chemical and Biological Warfare: A Comprehensive Survey for the Concerned Citizen.* New York: Copernicus, 2001.
Malcolm R. Dando	*Preventing Biological Warfare: The Failure of American Leadership.* New York: Palgrave Macmillan, 2002.
Janet M. Decker and J. Edward Alcamo, eds.	*Anthrax.* Broomall, PA: Chelsea House, 2003.
Erik de Clercq and Earl R. Kern, eds.	*Handbook of Viral Terrorism and Biodefense.* St. Louis, MO: Elsevier, 2003.
Editors of *The Doctors' Prescription for Healthy Living*	*Surviving Bioterrorism.* London: Freedom Press, 2003.
Bill Frist	*When Every Moment Counts: What You Need to Know About Bioterrorism from the Senate's Only Doctor.* Lanham, MD: Rowman & Littlefield, 2002.
David Heyman, Jerusha Achterberg, and Joelle Laszlo	*Lessons from the Anthrax Attacks: Implications for U.S. Bioterrorism Preparedness.* Washington, DC: Center for Strategic and International Studies, 2002.
Judith Miller, Stephen Engelberg, and William J. Broad	*Germs: Biological Weapons and America's Secret War.* New York: Simon & Schuster, 2001.
Marion Nestle	*Safe Food: Bacteria, Biotechnology, and Bioterror.* Berkeley: University of California Press, 2003.
Lloyd F. Novick and John S. Marr	*Public Health Issues in Disaster Preparedness: Focus on Bioterrorism.* Boston: Jones & Bartlett, 2003.
Gary Null and James Feast	*Germs, Biological Warfare, and Vaccinations: What You Need to Know.* New York: Seven Stories Press, 2003.

Michael T. Osterholm and John Schwartz	*Living Terrors: What America Needs to Know to Survive the Coming Bioterrorist Catastrophe.* New York: Delacorte, 2001.
Arthur P. Rogers, ed.	*Bioterrorism Reader.* Hauppauge, NY: Nova, 2003.
Alejandro E. Segarra	*Agroterrorism: Options for Congress.* Washington, DC: Congressional Research Service, 2001.
Wesley Shankland II	*Bioterrorism: You Can Survive.* Columbus, OH: AOmega, 2002.
Vickie Sutton	*Law and Bioterrorism.* Durham, NC: Carolina Academic Press, 2002.
Marilyn W. Thompson	*The Killer Strain: Anthrax and a Government Exposed.* New York: HarperCollins, 2003.
M. Sandra Wood, ed.	*Bioterrorism and Political Violence: Web Resources.* Binghamton, NY: Haworth, 2003.

Periodicals

Mark Alpert	"Spotty Defense: Big Cities Are Late to Vaccinate Against Smallpox," *Scientific American*, May 2003.
Guy F. Arnet	"What Can You Do to Protect Yourself Against Chemical, Biological, and Nuclear Terrorism?" *Backwoods Home Magazine*, May/June 2003.
BioScience	"Roundtable Examines Bioterrorism Threats to the Environment," May 2002.
Nell Boyce	"Keeping Details from the Devil," *U.S. News & World Report*, March 10, 2003.
Nell Boyce et al.	"Circle of Suspicion," *U.S. News & World Report*, August 26, 2002.
Shannon Brownlee	"Bad Reaction: The White House Stalls on Smallpox," *New Republic*, October 28, 2002.
Steve Bunk	"Bioterror in the Realm of Make-Believe," *Scientist*, June 10, 2002.
Steve Bunk	"Sensing Evil," *Scientist*, July 22, 2002.
Rocco Casagrande	"Technology Against Terror," *Scientific American*, October 2002.
Jon Cohen	"Designer Bugs," *Atlantic Monthly*, July/August, 2002.
Geoffrey Cowley	"The Plan to Fight Smallpox," *Newsweek*, October 14, 2002.
Madeline Drexler	"A Pox on America," *Nation*, April 28, 2003.
Economist	"The Spores of War: Biological Terrorism," November 30, 2002.
Economist	"Who Will Build Our Biodefenses? Vaccines Against Bioterrorism," February 1, 2003.

Sean Flynn   "What Ever Happened to Anthrax?" *Esquire*, March 2003.

Garance Franke-Ruta   "Homeland Security Is for Girls," *Washington Monthly*, April 2003.

Richard Gallagher   "Played Like a Fiddle on Bioterrorism," *Scientist*, April 7, 2003.

Scott Gottlieb   "Smallpox, Big Risk," *American Enterprise*, September 2002.

Judd Gregg   "Why America Needs Project BioShield," *Washington Times*, April 22, 2003.

Ricki Lewis   "Smallpox Vaccination: On Hold, but Lessons Learned," *Scientist*, July 8, 2002.

Stephen S. Morse   "The Vigilance Defense," *Scientific American*, October 2002.

Karen K. O'Brien,   "Recognition and Management of Bioterrorism
Mark Higdon, and   Infections," *American Family Physician*, May 1, 2003.
Jaime J. Halverson

N. Seppa   "Vaccine for All?" *Science News*, July 13, 2002.

Rachel Smolkin   "Thinking About the (No Longer) Unthinkable," *American Journalism Review*, May 2003.

Amanda Spake et al.   "Are You Ready?" *U.S. News & World Report*, February 24, 2003.

Nicholas Stix   "Media Manufacture Cloud of Suspicion over Hatfill," *Insight on the News*, August 12, 2002.

Index